easy
CONTAINER GARDENING

COLLINS

easy

CONTAINER GARDENING

Richard Jackson
&
Carolyn Hutchinson

HarperCollins*Publishers*

Acknowledgements

The publishers thank the following for their kind permission to
reproduce the photographs in this book:

Gillian Beckett pages 5 (bottom), 26 (bottom), 71 (top left and bottom), 78 (top),
82 (bottom right), 101 (top), 106 (left); **Deni Bown** pages 139 (top), 23 (bottom), 32 (bottom),
33 (bottom), 65, 93 (top), 97 (top); **Bob Gibbons Natural Image** pages 70 (top),
71 (top centre, top right), 80 (bottom), 80 (top right) (Liz Gibbons), 96 (bottom);
John Glover Photography pages 5 (third down), 8,11 (bottom), 12 (top left), 20, 21 (right), 25 (top),
27 (both), 28 (top and and bottom right), 31 (top), 34, 35, 36 (top), 37 (top), 39 (top),
42, 46, 53 (right), 54, 59 (right), 61, 62 (top), 63, 64, 66 (top), 68, 72, 73 (both), 74, 76 (top right),
77 (top), 79 (top), 83, 87, 89 (top left and bottom), 90 (bottom), 91 (top left), 92 (bottom),
95 (left), 97 (bottom), 98 (bottom), 100 (both), 102 (bottom); **Holt Studios International** pages 106 (right),
107 (both); **Hozelock** page 49; **Richard Jackson** page 23 (top); **Photos Horticultural
Picture Library** pages 29 (top right), 30 (top), 38 (top right), 39 (bottom), 44, 50, 52 (both),
58, 60, 67 (top), 70 (bottom), 75 (bottom left), 76 (top left), 77 (bottom), 78 (bottom), 79 (bottom),
81 (both), 82 (top), 84 (both), 85 (top), 86 (both), 88, 90 (top), 91 (top right and bottom), 92 (top),
93 (bottom), 94 (both), 95 (top), 96 (top), 98 (top), 99 (bottom), 101 (bottom), 102 (top), 103;
Graham Strong, Garden Folio pages 5 (second down), 14, 18 (bottom), 26 (top), 29 (top left),
31 (bottom), 32 (top), 35 (top left), 47, 51, 53 (left), 85 (bottom); **Textice Ltd** page 45 (both);
Vernons Geranium Nursery page 55 (both).

All other photographs supplied by *Garden Answers* magazine.

First published in hardback as *How to Win at Container Gardening* in 1996
by HarperCollins*Publishers*, London
This paperback edition first published in 1999

A CIP catalogue record for this book is available from the British Library

ISBN 0 00 414 058 3

Designed and produced by Cooling Brown

Colour reproduction by Colourscan, Singapore
Printed and bound in Italy by Rotolito Lombarda SpA, Milan

Contents

INTRODUCTION

THE GREAT THING about growing plants in pots is that there is always room for one more! This book provides perfect solutions for every position and purpose, from food in pots to colourful mixed containers and show-stopping shrubs. There's a section on hanging baskets and window boxes which will delight with ideas for winter and spring schemes as well as those for summer. There's practical advice on planting up, plus plenty of expert tips on how to keep plants in peak condition and the book deals with problem solving in a down-to-earth manner. An important section of the book devoted to Top Plants lists the authors' favourite and most reliable container species.

ADRIENNE WILD
(Editor, *Garden Answers* magazine)

Pots and Tubs

It's no wonder that gardening in pots, tubs, troughs and planters is so popular. Virtually anything, from a majestic clipped bay tree to a humble clump of snowdrops, will happily thrive for years in a pot. In fact, simply by providing the right conditions, you'll find that you can succeed with an amazing range of plants, including those that wouldn't like your garden soil but will flourish in a pot if you give them the right compost.

Whatever you decide to grow, you'll find that the secrets of success are pretty straightforward. Most plants just need decent compost, a bit of sun, regular watering and occasional feeding. And it honestly doesn't matter what type of container you use, whether it's a battered old paint can with holes in the bottom or a sumptuous handmade terracotta pot. But each material has its own particular advantages (and disadvantages), so make your choice with care.

CHOOSING CONTAINERS
TERRACOTTA

The warm brown colour of terracotta pots looks beautifully natural in any situation, so it's not surprising that they are the most popular of all. Available in a glorious selection of shapes, sizes and styles – from the standard no-nonsense flowerpot to ornate planters festooned with swags, garlands and chirpy cherubs there's a terracotta pot for every conceivable plant and situation.

What's more, they look even better as they get older, their rich tones mellowing very gracefully over the years. And, aesthetics aside, they're also good news from the plant's point of view because, being porous, they are far less likely to get waterlogged in winter.

But terracotta is brittle and breaks easily, so should be handled with care and kept out of the way of rampaging children and dogs. And some of the less well-made pots (those fired in the kiln at lower temperatures) aren't frostproof and can shatter in a hard winter. Most reputable companies do now guarantee their pots against frost damage, so check the label carefully before you buy.

Pots of choice come in all shapes and sizes and from the plainest to the most decorative. Patterns may be embossed, glazed or even hand-painted.

The earthy glow of terracotta provides the perfect setting for container plantings.

Until a few years ago, the other major disadvantage with terracotta pots was their cost; they could be horrendously expensive. But prices for machine-made pots have plummeted recently and there are some real bargains to be found at garden centres and DIY superstores. Even some of the handmade pots are better value now, especially those imported from China. The beautiful handmade English pots still cost a fortune, but the craftsmanship that goes into them makes them the most desirable of all.

And just a word on the curvaceous Ali Baba pots. They're especially vulnerable to frost, because when the compost freezes and expands, the neck of the jar prevents it from moving upwards as it would in a normal pot. In addition, vigorous plants which have become potbound are virtually impossible to remove because the solid rootball won't pass through the narrow neck. So to avoid breakages or repotting problems, use Ali Baba pots or oil jars for summer plantings only, or leave them entirely unplanted as a decorative feature in their own right.

PLASTIC

The basic rule with plastic pots is that you get what you pay for. The cheapest are understandably the most popular, but they don't last long; they get brittle in the sun and will eventually crack. The more expensive plastic pots are thicker and stronger and their lifespan is much longer.

There's an excellent range of styles to choose from, but you'll find the colours far less exciting. Avoid white at all costs. It's too bright to begin with and sticks out like a sore thumb, then it gets grubby as it ages and is impossible to keep looking clean. Black is rather too functional, and absorbs heat in a sunny spot, which could harm the plants' roots. Green and brown are the safe choices.

There's also a range of ornamental terracotta look-alike plastic pots, and the better ones are pretty convincing. They are a good, and slightly cheaper, alternative to real terracotta for both balcony and rooftop gardens where weight is a crucial factor and pots need to be as light as possible.

A wooden trug, lined with polythene, can be used to house a spectacular short-term display of spring alpines.

PLANTING IN GROWBAGS

Growbags were originally developed for commercial tomato growers, but rapidly became popular with amateur gardeners. They're ideal for tomatoes and other crops such as peppers and aubergines in the greenhouse or in a sunny spot outdoors.

Of all the forms of container gardening, these are by far the best value for money, and many people buy them for the compost alone and use it in pots and window boxes.

To get the best results, growbags should never be allowed to dry out, and in high summer this can mean watering at least once a day. Bulrush's Easi-Grow system (a water reservoir supplying moisture to the growbag) need only be topped up every fortnight or so, promoting strong, even growth.

If, like us, you find the bright patterns on the bags a bit distracting, disguise them by placing a few small pots of bedding plants or herbs around the edge. Alternatively, add a few seeds of nasturtium or a couple of trailing lobelias when planting. They'll soon cover the garish plastic.

Growbags are just as useful for bedding plants as they are for tomatoes – be sure to include a few trailers to hide the brightly coloured plastic!

WOOD

Another natural choice, wooden containers look attractive and give good insulation too, providing protection against cold in winter and hot sun in summer. However the range is rather limited to half barrels and tubs, unless you fancy making your own.

When choosing a half barrel, check that any timber preservatives used on it were of the non-toxic kind (incredibly, some people still use plant-killing creosote). Check, too, that the staves are secure, and not loose or rattly. Barrels that have been allowed to dry out will shrink, and there's a danger of the whole thing falling apart the minute you get it home. Similarly, if you're not planting up immediately, either fill it with compost anyway, or hose it down occasionally, to keep the wood moist and fully expanded.

To extend its life, treat the outside of the barrel with a non-toxic timber preservative every year. Standing it on tiles or bricks will help drainage and prevent the base from rotting.

A wooden half barrel makes a sympathetic container for a spring planting of daffodils with a skirt of ivy around them.

The symmetry of this finely detailed stone trough is echoed by the formal planting.

Ceramic pots planted up in the oriental style – the quiet 'rock' garden in particular – would be quick and easy to recreate.

STONE

Concrete planters are the least expensive of the 'stone' tubs. They are long-lasting, provide good insulation to protect plant roots against winter cold, and are very solid looking. Many people, however, prefer the more natural appearance of the reconstituted stone containers which look more like the real thing, at a fraction of the cost. Made from a mix of concrete and crushed stone, it's cast in a good range of shapes, sizes and muted colours. For a large, decorative container with a high quality finish and fine detailing, it's difficult to beat reconstituted stone.

GLAZED CERAMICS

These oriental-style pots are good value but should be chosen with care, since those with bold patterns of bamboo leaves or dragons can look out of place in, say, a cottage garden setting, where the plain blue or green pots would be a safer bet. All of them are useful for bringing an exotic and slightly different touch to the

garden, and they look especially good when planted with bamboo or, in a shady spot, with one of the Japanese maples.

FIBRE PLANTERS

These have a peat-like colour and texture and are made from compressed fibre. They are cheap, light and biodegradable, but will only last a couple of years or so. And as they're not particularly attractive, use trailing plants to soften their impact. Best used for a mass display of summer bedding or inside a more decorative pot.

Functional but less than beautiful, fibre planters look best when hidden by plants.

UNUSUAL CONTAINERS

Almost anything can be pressed into service as a plant container so long as it can hold compost and has good drainage. One of the best ideas is one we've borrowed from the doyenne of container gardening, Kathleen Brown; wicker baskets make lovely containers, especially for spring bulbs, and if you paint them with three coats of polyurethane varnish they'll last for years.

We've also seen wonderful results using leaky old boots, paint cans, oil drums and recycled kitchen pots of various kinds. So have a bit of fun with your containers. If nothing else, it'll give you, your friends and your neighbours a good laugh.

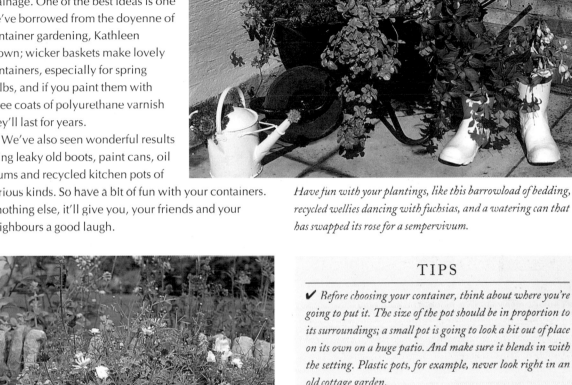

Have fun with your plantings, like this barrowload of bedding, recycled wellies dancing with fuchsias, and a watering can that has swapped its rose for a sempervivum.

Wicker baskets look lovely in a garden setting and can last for years if protected by several coats of varnish.

TIPS

✔ *Before choosing your container, think about where you're going to put it. The size of the pot should be in proportion to its surroundings; a small pot is going to look a bit out of place on its own on a huge patio. And make sure it blends in with the setting. Plastic pots, for example, never look right in an old cottage garden.*

✔ *The colour of brand new stone or terracotta pots can be softened by painting them with natural yoghurt or dilute manure. This almost-instant aging treatment encourages the growth of algae and lichen.*

✔ *Plant towers are an ingenious way of growing lots of flowers, strawberries or herbs in a column and a number of different free-standing models are available. The results can be spectacular, but take care when watering — it's important that the plants at the bottom of the tower get enough water.*

✔ *In really hot spots, it's worth lining the inside (but not the base) of terracotta pots with polythene before planting, to prevent moisture from evaporating through the porous clay.*

✔ *Chimney pots can be highly decorative and while you can simply wedge a planted plastic pot in the top, you'll give plants a much better root run if you use bricks or rubble as a drainage layer and fill up the rest of the chimney pot with potting compost.*

Growing Success

Container plants are a bit like babies. They rely entirely on you for every aspect of their lives: food, drink, comfortable compost for their roots, the right amount of sun or shade. But provided you plant them properly and treat them well, they'll be bouncing and bonny – a real credit to your fostering skills.

WHICH POTTING COMPOST?

'The answer lies in the soil' goes the old gardening saying, meaning that if you get the soil right, your plants will flourish. And it's just as true for gardening in pots as it is for open-ground plantings.

It's essential that you use potting compost for your pots and tubs. Garden soil just won't do: in pot conditions it becomes airless and compacted, and can harbour diseases and pests; potted plants hate it. It's an expensive operation initially, especially if you're faced with a cavernous half-barrel, but vital for success. So grit your teeth, dig deep in your pocket and give your plants the growing conditions they deserve.

But which type of compost to use? They're made to different recipes, to suit different groups of plants, so take your pick from the following:

Multipurpose/universal composts

These composts are normally based on peat, and the advantages are that they're light (useful for balcony gardeners), clean to handle, and moisture-retentive. The disadvantage is that when they do dry out completely, they can be difficult to re-wet (see 'Watering'). And we don't recommend them for spring-flowering bulbs which are wintered outdoors – in cold, wet spells, the soil retains rather too much moisture and this can encourage rotting.

Scarlet geraniums and the most strikingly coloured of all pansies, 'Jolly Joker', dominate this grouping of summer pots.

Especially useful for: bedding plants; vegetables; strawberries; summer bulbs. Can also be used for most permanent plants, but not quite as nutrient-rich as John Innes composts.

John Innes

All the John Innes composts are soil-based and therefore rather heavier to handle. They also contain peat and sand, so that they retain moisture without becoming waterlogged. The amount of nutrients in each type varies from low-nutrient John Innes No 1 which is used for cuttings and seedlings, through medium-strong John Innes No 2, to super-rich John Innes No 3 for maturer plants which appreciate a substantial diet.

Use John Innes No 2 for: herbs; young trees, shrubs and climbers; most conifers; hardy perennials like hostas and ferns; roses; fruit; vegetables; spring bulbs.

Use John Innes No 3 for: mature trees, shrubs and climbers; climbing roses.

Ericaceous compost

Ericaceous compost is peat-based and specially formulated for acid-loving, lime-hating plants.

Main uses: rhododendrons; azaleas; camellias; magnolias; pieris. A few other plants, that don't fall into any broad category, are noted as ericaceous when we describe them.

Use broken pieces of terracotta as a drainage layer to prevent compost from blocking up the single drainage hole in clay pots. Fill up with compost, mixing in a slow-release fertilizer at the recommended rate to keep plants well fed all season. Set the plants in the compost at their previous planting level.

GROWING SUCCESS

PREPARATION AND PLANNING

Step 1: Come clean

Cleaning out pots and tubs between planting is one of the muckiest, most boring jobs in the world. But it is important because unwashed containers can harbour pests and diseases. Just take, for instance, the eggs of the

dreaded vine weevil (see Problem Solving, p. 106).
They're minute, and they could be lurking in that little scraping of compost at the bottom of the pot, ready to hatch and launch a vicious onslaught on your precious (and costly) plants.

Happily, you needn't worry so much about the exterior of terracotta and stone pots. With age, they take on a lovely weathered patina, and those lichened surfaces are totally benign and very attractive.

Step 2: Good drainage

Unless you're growing water plants, you have to make sure that excess water can drain away easily from your pots and tubs, otherwise the compost can become stagnant and cause fatal root-rotting.

To prevent compost from blocking up the drainage holes, place a layer of drainage material at the bottom of the pot: 13mm/½in of gravel or small garden stones is fine for smaller plastic pots, up to 5cm/2in in larger ones. The single drainage hole that's the norm for most terracotta pots can be protected by placing two or three crocks (broken pieces of pot, curved side uppermost) over it. But if you're fresh out of broken pots, a layer of gravel or stones will do the same job. In containers such as half-barrels with a large base to cover, use a 7.5-15cm/3-6in layer of crocks, large stones, broken brick or any other garden rubble.

Step 3: Planting

Once you've created the drainage layer, fill up with your chosen compost to the point where the base of the plant will sit. Fill in round the plant, taking care not to leave any substantial air pockets and firm it in. Level off the compost at 2.5-5cm/1-2in below the rim, depending on

---

TIPS

✔ *Most garden centres and DIY stores use growbags as a 'loss-leader' to entice you in. The compost from growbags is, therefore, the cheapest of all the multipurpose types, and is perfectly good for bedding plants, strawberries and smaller vegetables such as lettuces and dwarf beans.*

✔ *Placing saucers under pots does conserve water in summer for moisture-lovers like hostas, but with other plants you run the risk of waterlogging unless you're prepared to empty away excess water once they've had a good drink.*

✔ *John Innes composts are useful where weight is a positive advantage. Lilies, for instance, can be top-heavy plants, and a plastic pot will be more securely anchored by John Innes than by the lighter multipurpose composts.*

✔ *As an added guarantee of success, choose plants that are healthy and happy to start with. Bulbs should be fat and firm, and any that have sprouted excessively, or have started to go mouldy, should be rejected. For all other plants, choose those with sturdy stems and shapely, vigorous growth. Reject any with spindly, drawn growth, any sign of pest or disease, completely dry compost, or excessive amounts of root emerging from the drainage holes.*

the size of the pot, to allow room for watering.

All plants should be watered well after planting, and it's especially important to keep them watered through any dry spells until they start to establish and put on new growth.

The actual planting technique varies slightly, so here's a quick run-down of the main types:

Bulbs should, generally, be planted at three times their own height. Therefore a 5cm/2in high bulb will need a hole 15cm/6in deep. Any less and you risk them coming up 'blind' – plenty of healthy leaves but not a flower in sight.

Water **container-grown plants** a while before planting, to make it easier to remove them from their pots. Gently tease out any roots that are growing in circles round the rootball, and fan them out. If you don't, they'll carry on growing in circles and never become firmly anchored in the compost. Fill in so that the top of the original soil is level with the fresh compost.

Soak **bare-root plants** (such as the roses and small trees that are available in autumn) in a bucket of water for an hour before planting. Mound up the compost in the centre of the container, then sit the plant in and spread out the roots before filling in. Roses should be planted so that the knobbly junction between roots and stems is 2.5cm/1in below the surface. A dark mark made by the soil on tree stems indicates the original level at which it was planted.

Trees will need staking for the first two years, unless the garden is very sheltered. So as you're planting, plunge the stake deep into the compost, with only the top 60cm/2ft above soil level, and attach it to the tree with an adjustable tree tie.

Climbers which are intended for a trellis on a backing wall should be gently ushered in the right direction by tying them in to angled canes, using soft garden twine.

FEEDING

All plants need food, and the need is even greater in containers where the roots aren't free to roam in search of fresh supplies. Potting composts come ready-charged with nutrients, but they can't be relied on to last for more than six to eight weeks. After that, it's up to you. But how often to feed, and with what? Plants vary in their feeding habits, so here's a breakdown of the major groups.

And just a final reminder – fresh compost contains plant food. So don't feed plants during the first six weeks or they'll get indigestion.

Greedy feeders

These are the plants that put all their efforts into one short season. Summer annuals and bedding plants, flowering prolifically for months on end, need regular help after they've exhausted the nutrients in the compost. A weekly feed of liquid tomato food will keep them going nicely.

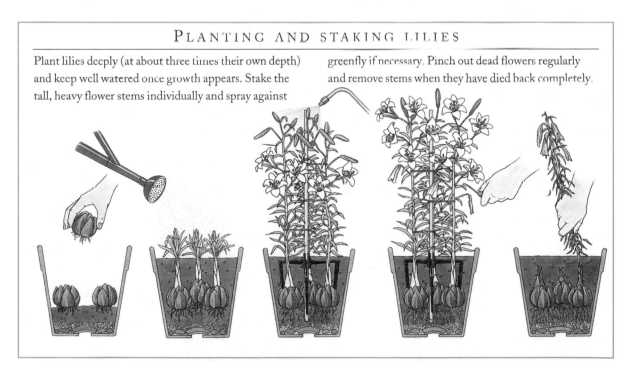

PLANTING AND STAKING LILIES

Plant lilies deeply (at about three times their own depth) and keep well watered once growth appears. Stake the tall, heavy flower stems individually and spray against greenfly if necessary. Pinch out dead flowers regularly and remove stems when they have died back completely.

An inverted plastic bottle with holes in the cap, inserted in the compost, delivers water and feed directly to the plants' roots.

Vigorous fruits and fruiting vegetables such as tomatoes, cucumbers and courgettes will also appreciate liquid tomato food. Wait until the first tiny fruits are forming, then start to feed weekly.

Sensible eaters

Plants that plod along in a relatively undemanding way include trees, shrubs, roses, climbers and hardy perennials. Feed them with a general liquid fertilizer in early spring and again in May and mid-July.

Smaller vegetables such as lettuce and dwarf beans will need a feed of general liquid fertilizer every couple of weeks.

Bread and water dieters

Most herbs, alpines and decorative succulent plants like stonecrops (sedums) need very little feeding. But if they start to lose vigour, give them a half-strength dose of general liquid fertilizer in early spring.

Bulbs, too, need little food, since they manufacture their own from the leaves. But they do appreciate a couple of doses of liquid tomato food after flowering, to enable them to build up their strength for the following year's flowers.

Choosy eaters

Ericaceous plants (the lime-haters that we've listed under 'Ericaceous compost', above) benefit greatly from a special ericaceous feed, such as Miracle Garden Care Miracid, given in early spring. This boosts the acidity of the potting compost and feeds the plants at the same time.

WATERING

Watering is the most time-consuming chore in container gardening – smaller pots may need to be watered twice a day in very hot weather. Automatic watering systems will do the job for you but it's an expensive option and it's hard to hide the resultant 'spaghetti junction' of pipes.

How often to water? The scientific answer is 'It depends on the weather.' Pots and tubs can be allowed to become fairly dry between waterings, but you can run into trouble if you let them dry out completely. John Innes composts aren't difficult to re-wet, but the peat-based types can be a nightmare. The compost shrinks away from the side of the pot and water simply pours over the bone-dry surface and down the gap between pot and compost. Plunge smaller containers in a water-filled bucket or sink until the rootball is thoroughly saturated. Larger pots can be re-wetted by watering from a can fitted with a rose, or a hose fitted with a sprayer. This artificial rain penetrates more easily than a solid stream of water.

So try to keep your containers evenly moist but not sodden, giving them a good drink when they need it, rather than a surface sprinkling. Don't assume they've been watered if it's been raining: the foliage in densely planted pots can deflect rain, leaving the compost dry.

The regular removal of spent blooms ensures a continuous succession of flower and prevents plants from going to seed.

A NEW LEASE OF LIFE FOR A BROKEN POT

Accidents will happen, especially as a result of frost damage , and terracotta pots are expensive – so it's good to do a rescue job if at all possible. A little ingenuity has turned this bowl-shaped pot, broken but not damaged beyond salvation, into an attractive and unusual container for an alpine planting.

1 Crock the pot and fill in with John Innes No 2 compost, with added grit to provide the sharp drainage alpines need.

2 Heap the compost in the unbroken portion, using the broken piece as a retaining wall. Set in the first 3 plants.

3 Pack compost into the remaining lower level, and set in trailing and cushion-forming plants to soften the broken edge.

4 A layer of gravel around the plants provides the final touch: it looks decorative and gives sharper drainage.

The finished pot, looking as though it was meant to be like this all along, provides a carefully thought out and beautifully constructed miniature landscape on two levels. Placed in a sunny spot, it will give pleasure for a good many years.

ROUTINE CARE

Remove any **weeds** before they get a hold and start to compete with the plants for water and nutrients.

Deadhead regularly – all plants, and especially bedding plants, will flower much more vigorously if you pick off faded blooms.

Woody plants will need occasional **pruning** to keep them healthy, productive and within their alloted space. Timing and methods vary widely, and any good reference book will help you out.

Permanent plants such as trees, shrubs, fruit and hardy perennials will need **repotting** from time to time as they outgrow their pots. Signs to look for are decreasing vigour, and a mass of congested roots in the pot. Tease these roots out as much as you can before transferring the plant to a pot one size bigger. Once plants reach maturity and no longer need repotting, refresh the compost each spring by **top-dressing** it.

This simply means scraping away the top layer of compost and replacing it with fresh. Similarly, when replanting tubs which are used primarily for seasonal bedding, remove the top 7.5cm/3in of compost and replace with a fresh layer.

If you are growing slightly tender plants such as cordylines and bays, they may need some **winter protection** unless you live in a very mild district. If hard frosts are forecast, draping the containers with horticultural fleece (or even old net curtains) should do the trick. Evergreen shrubs and trees are the most vulnerable if the compost in the pots freezes up for long periods – they're unable to take up the moisture that sustains the leaves – but even deciduous plants are at risk if the root system is frozen for long periods. So in colder areas, wrap plastic and terracotta containers in bubble plastic whenever hard frosts are forecast.

SUMMER SPECTACULAR

Making the most of the
Summer Spectacular

The only problem with summer plants in pots and tubs is getting them to <u>stop</u> growing. They're coming at you from all sides: roses demanding to be admired, lilies rushing into bloom, continental geraniums shooting out starbursts of flower, fuchsias dripping with ballerina blossoms. It's a hectic, wonderful time of year. It becomes a labour of love, too, as you patiently deadhead, feed and water. But you will be magnificently repaid.

THE BEDDING BONANZA

Keen container gardeners get really itchy-fingered in April – because they know that, come May, and the last of the spring frosts, they can get down to some seriously colourful gardening. Bedding plants are such incredible value for money, flowering their hearts out for month after month. And all credit to the breeders (even though we sometimes snap at them for their wilder fantasies like pink daffodils) for making them ever more reliable and weather resistant. Ever more compact, too – a wonderful asset for container gardening, provided that the plant doesn't become just too dumpy and lose its original character.

BUYING EARLY

If you have the space, it's well worth buying plug or mini-plant bedding in late March or early April, potting them up and growing them on in a warm, light spot indoors. By the time you put them out in late May or early June they'll be sturdy, well-grown plants for instant impact at minimal cost.

Some garden centres actually start selling these plants in February, but we don't recommend that you buy them this early unless you have a cool, frost-free and very light spot indoors in which to grow them. Plants brought into the warmth of the house in late winter when light levels are low can become tall and

A tiny courtyard garden bursts with bright colour from the rich variety of beautifully tended bedding plants.

Fuchsias really give of their best if they're provided with a deep, moist root run in a generous container.

spindly. And don't forget to harden your plants off – get them used to the lower night temperatures of the garden – before you put them outside permanently. A couple of weeks before they're due to go out, stand them outdoors in a warm sheltered spot during the day and bring them in at night. In the second week, leave them outside round the clock, unless frost is forecast.

SUMMER SPECTACULAR

PINK AND CREAM CONFECTION

Looking almost good enough to eat, this planting combines soft, luminous colours to tremendous effect. The salmon-pink and candyfloss-pink trumpets of nicotiana and petunia blend beautifully with the palest gold daisies of argyranthemum (marguerite) and osteospermum in a 45cm/18in pot.

INGREDIENTS
- 2 x *Osteospermum* 'Buttermilk'
- 4 x *Nicotiana* 'Domino Salmon Pink'
- 4 x *Petunia* 'Celebrity Ovation'
- 1 x *Argyranthemum* 'Peach Cheeks' (centre)

❧ *If you can't find* Petunia *'Celebrity Ovation', pictured here, use 'Chiffon Morn' which is more widely available in plant and seed form.*

DESIGNING WITH BEDDING PLANTS

You don't, of course, have to have any preplanned design at all for your bedding plants. Just cram your pots to overflowing with fuchsias and geraniums, let bright nasturtiums ramp, plant up lots of electrically luminous tuberous begonias in clashing colours, allow petunias to blow their own trumpets as loudly as possible. In other words, go mad, break all the design rules and have a ball. You'll find that, so long as there's enough contrast of plant heights, shapes and textures, you've created a quite delightful jumble which, if you've a mind, you can airily describe as 'cottage gardening'.

More cautious souls, though, might like to stick to safer, tried and tested formulas when combining bedding plants in pots and tubs. Pink, white and blue is one such formula, and you'll never go wrong with it – a large pot containing a pale pink fuchsia like the frilly, delightfully named 'Devonshire Dumpling', a couple of upright white geraniums and an infill of blue lobelia will be dreamily beautiful all summer long. Blue with lemon or gold won't let you down either, and you could add a touch of white to keep it really cool and crisp. Stronger, hotter colours are harder to match up, but crimson and deep purple are a safe bet, and clear reds (with no hint of pink) can look stunning with orange. Or you could just leave it to the nurserymen, many of whom now supply exceedingly tasteful colour-themed collections of plug plants.

You can also choose to use summer containers as 'props' in the garden, rather than confining them to the patio. In a really tiny garden, for instance, that's colour-themed in white, silver and green for a tranquil picture, summer pots of white petunias, standard marguerites and, in shady spots, white busy lizzies can be given centre stage in May and will add immensely to the garden's charms through summer. Or choose a quiet corner of the garden with a predominantly green backdrop and install an ornate urn or terracotta pot planted with an eruption of colour. Steps, too, make a wonderful home for pots of bedding and even the dullest set of concrete treads and risers can be turned into an asset if it's flanked by generously planted pots. One of the great joys of bedding plants in pots is the flights of fancy that you can achieve!

THE CONTAINED HERB GARDEN

A contained herb garden, in its full midsummer glory, is a happy place to be on a sunny day. Pull up a chair and immerse yourself in a world of scents from the sharpest to the sweetest, enjoy the tall, feathery foliage of fennel, contrasting beautifully with a neat dome of grey-green sage. Close your eyes as this outdoor aromatherapy starts to relax you, and listen to the murmur of bees blundering, heavy laden, through the flowers of thyme and rosemary. Wonderful. But if this is the sort of mini herb garden you dream of, it needs a little planning.

LOVE ME TENDER

Two of the most striking plants for urns, pots and tubs are cordyline and phormium, which make wonderfully architectural specimens to highlight a particular garden feature (a flight of steps for instance), or to contrast with softer plantings nearby. But they are both tender (though phormiums will survive outdoors in very mild areas in the south and west), so bring them under cover for the winter; a frost-free greenhouse or conservatory is ideal.

Cordyline australis makes a lush fountain of narrow leaves on an ever-lengthening trunk, and purple-flushed 'Purpurea' is an especially good form, slowly growing to 1.5m/5ft or more. *Phormium tenax* is more solidly dramatic, with iris-like clumps of tall, sword-shaped leaves to around 90cm/3ft. Again, the coloured forms are the most desirable, like bronze-purple 'Purpureum', or 'Sundowner', a smoky grey, edged with pink.

Bronzy phormiums glow in low evening sun, their spiky leaves making a dramatic contrast with surrounding plants.

Choice of pots first. Few herbs trail to any great extent, so your container will be almost as much in the limelight as the plants. And we recommend that (so far as you can afford it) you use natural materials. The warm tones and earthy finish of terracotta, plain or fancy, looks absolutely right, with stone or reconstituted stone a close second. Wood looks good, too, and a full-sized barrel would accommodate enough plants to keep even the most herb-mad cook in rich pickings. On the minus side, glazed ceramic pots are a bit too bright for the subtle colours of a herb garden, while plastic pots look even more out of place and can heat up alarmingly in the sunny spots that most herbs prefer.

If you've any money left after we've bullied you into spending a small fortune on pots, it's time to think about the plants to incorporate in your scheme. The basic culinary herbs will be top of your list – the 'Scarborough Fair' parsley, sage, rosemary and thyme types. But go for the best, most interesting forms for both flavour and good looks. Strongly-flavoured flat-leaved parsley, for instance, instead of the chewy moss curled types.

Variegated sages, golden thymes, bronze fennel, French tarragon, a wonderful rosemary like 'Benenden Blue' which, instead of growing formally upright, will cascade down the side of a container. And track down some of the more unusual culinary herbs. Sweet cicely, for example, with soft, downy leaves, looks rather like cow parsley and has a strong, sweet aniseed flavour. Grow rocket, for a delicious mix of nuttiness, oiliness

Everything is to hand here for the happy cook – a wide selection of herbs for the main course and fresh strawberries for dessert.

SUMMER SPECTACULAR

REFRESHING YELLOW AND WHITE

Crisp lemon and white form the basis of this planting in a 50cm/20in pot, giving a fresh, cool feel with just a touch of warmth from the marigolds. The pale gold leaves of *Lamium* 'Gold Nugget' can just be seen peeping through on the left.

INGREDIENTS
• 3 x French marigold 'Royal King'
• 1 x *Lamium* 'Gold Nugget'
• 2 x *Bacopa* 'Snowflake'
• 2 x *Petunia* 'Surfinia White'
• 3 x *Argyranthemum* 'Lemon Meringue'

❀ *If the 'Lemon Meringue' is hard to find, both 'Cornish Gold' and 'Jamaica Primrose' would make excellent substitutes.*

❀ *Be sure to choose one of the taller varieties of marigold that can cope with the exuberance of the other plants.*

and spiciness. And have you tried garlic chives? They have flattened reed-like leaves, pretty white flowers and a delicate garlic/onion taste. Or Welsh onions, with fat tubular leaves that are brilliant for adding to a stir fry at the last minute. And if you're a complete foodie, how about growing your own lemon grass? It's not hardy, so give it a 25cm/10in pot in a sunny spot in summer and overwinter it in a warm light spot indoors. It's not widely available either, but you'll find a number of suppliers listed under its Latin name of *Cymbopogon citratus* in the plant-hunter's bible, *The Plant Finder*.

Now that you've gathered together all the ingredients for your herb garden, it only remains to plant them up and set them outdoors in a sheltered, sunny spot; very few herbs, mint apart, will thrive in shade. Cluster the pots together to make the most of the contrasting colours, shapes and textures of the plants. And pull up that chair we were talking about at the beginning.

POTTED FRUIT AND VEGETABLES
If you've a passion for fresh-picked fruit and veg but you're stumped for garden space, then pots and tubs are your answer. There's a tremendous range that you can grow, from juicy apples to luscious tomatoes and fiery chilli peppers.

Concentrate on the really worthwhile varieties; flavour and speed and ease of cropping are the first priorities, with shop prices a close runner-up – it would be pointless to devote space to, say, a potato barrel planted up with late varieties which you'll be harvesting just when they're at their cheapest at the greengrocer's. And some fruit and veg just aren't suitable for, or don't like, container culture, so the following …

FRUIT	VEGETABLES
blackberries	asparagus
blackcurrants	broccoli
gooseberries	cabbages
grapes	cauliflowers
loganberries	celery
other hybrid berries	leeks
raspberries	marrows
redcurrants	parsnips
white currants	sprouts

… are best avoided. Although you're very welcome to have a go and prove us wrong!

A sunny spot is, of course, essential for almost all fruits and vegetables, and in most cases they'll be sharing it with permanent potted plants and with pots of

Strawberries in pots are basking and ripening in the sun. This variety, 'Gorella', yields early, well-flavoured crops.

you will have injected a bit of drama into the picture.

Sweet peppers, too, are tremendously ornamental, with colours ranging from the traditional red and green to black, yellow and orange. The same goes for red or green chilli peppers, which thrive outdoors in a sheltered spot in warm areas. There's an especially hot variety called 'Hero'.

And if you want to really jazz things up, use a haze of lobelias as an underplanting for your potted apples, let a bright orange nasturtium wander through your courgettes, tuck a few red busy lizzies in a tomato pot. 'Potager' gardening – growing flowers and food together – is tremendously popular and your crops are better protected from pests; they don't home in on a mixed planting quite so readily, because the mix of scents confuses their radar.

colourful summer bedding. So buy the most decorative varieties, that will fit easily into the scene. Fruit trees are naturally attractive, and both the leaves and fruit of strawberries are very pretty, but some of the vegetables lack a certain oomph. If you're growing lettuces in a growbag, for instance, ten plants in the same plain green will look a bit agricultural. But if you add a few looseleaf lettuces like 'Lollo Rossa', with its deep red frilly leaves,

SITTING PRETTY IN PINK

This open, airy planting uses delicate trailers that won't hide the attractive 45cm/16in terracotta look-alike pedestal. By July, the penstemons will be in full bloom to add the finishing touch to this softly coloured, romantic scheme.

INGREDIENTS
• 2 x *Penstemon* 'Hidcote Pink'
• 2 x *Penstemon* 'Heavenly Blue'
• 3 x *Petunia* 'Celebrity Encore' series
• 1 x *Verbena* 'Sissinghurst Pink'
• 1 x *Scaevola*

❀ *When filling this planter with compost, be sure to pack it right in round the hollow of the curved base.*

❀ *To keep the penstemons from year to year, take cuttings in August.*

Making the most of Permanent Plantings

The shrubs planted in a collection of containers – here, pieris and euonymus – help to give structure to the grouping.

It's wonderful to fill patios and balconies with lashings of colourful spring bulbs and summer bedding plants. But it's the permanent plants that give the area its atmosphere and its structure. Use trees, shrubs and climbers for the basic framework, with hardy perennials of all shapes and sizes to plug the gaps.

Permanent plants will give a fully planted, settled feel to any area where pots and tubs predominate, especially if you use a good proportion of evergreens to maintain the structure through the winter. And while some will be simply a foliage foil for summer plantings, others, like roses and camellias, will contribute their own colour.

TREES, SHRUBS AND CLIMBERS

Don't be scared of growing trees in large pots and tubs. All but the most vigorous will live very happily in a container so long as they're well fed and watered,

EVERGOLDS

Evergreen shrubs with golden foliage or leaves with gold variegation are tremendous value, providing a sunny backdrop for summer schemes and a focus of cheery colour in winter. *Elaeagnus* x *ebbingei* 'Limelight' (1.5m/5ft) is especially good, the dark green leathery leaves generously splashed with a subtle mix of gold and pale green. Rather neater at 60cm/2ft is *Euonymus fortunei* 'Emerald 'n' Gold', a mass of small gold-edged leaves that take on a pink tinge in winter.

And for a formal feature, gold-variegated hollies (*Ilex*) look marvellous clipped into pyramids or cones. 'Golden King' is relatively spineless – useful when placing a potted holly close to a narrow path – and, being a female (the naming of hollies is less than straightforward), will set a good crop of berries if there's a male holly nearby. 'Golden Queen' would do nicely.

Choisya ternata 'Sundance' is another beautiful evergold.

Acer palmatum dissectum *(a form of Japanese maple) is a wonderfully elegant small tree for dappled shade.*

The fiery autumn tints of Spiraea *'Golden Princess' echo the tawny gold chrysanthemums and the rose-purple* Erica gracilis.

though they're unlikely to reach the same height and spread as they would if planted in the garden. Take the Chelsea Flower Show gardens as your inspiration – most of the mature trees on display there are grown in large pots, for portability, and sunk into the ground. And year after year those same trees in those same pots, return to the show for a sparkling repeat performance.

Any tree that's listed as having an ultimate height of around 7.5m/25ft is a possibility, which gives you a tremendous range to choose from. There's also a wealth of small 'patio' trees, like the tiny (1.8m/6ft) *Salix caprea* 'Kilmarnock', which are naturals for tubs. Then there are conifers, which provide evergreen colour and structure and are especially good for a formal setting because of their densely clothed, symmetrical shapes. You can cheat, too, and turn other types of plants into trees by training them as standards. The shrub *Fatsia japonica* responds well to this treatment, as does the Japanese wisteria, *Wisteria floribunda*; both should do well in 60cm/2ft barrels. The trick is to take out all sideshoots as the main stem grows, until you have a clear 1.8m/6ft trunk. The head of the plant will then bush out into an extremely attractive 'tree'.

When it comes to shrubs, all, from the smallest to the very largest, can be pressed into service as potted plants. This gives you access to everything from tiny hebes to rhododendrons, azaleas, camellias, shrubby magnolias, shrub roses, pieris, and even the rampant *Lavatera* 'Barnsley' with its mass of pale pink flowers for weeks on end. And don't overlook the value of those that are grown solely for the beauty of their foliage, and the virtues of evergreens that give such pleasure in winter.

Container-grown climbers are invaluable for the many houses that are completely marooned in a concrete surround. Install a couple of tubs and those blank walls will soon be swathed in colour from ivies, clematis, roses, creepers, honeysuckles and a host of other lovelies. Summer jasmine is the ideal climber for clothing a pergola: it'll romp away and its starry flowers and sweet scent guarantee many enchanted evenings.

FABULOUS FOLIAGE

The incredible variety of shape, colour and texture of leaves can be every bit as exciting as flowers in the contained garden. Take *Acer palmatum* 'Dissectum Atropurpureum' for example, which is a ghastly

An eye-catching grouping of ornamental grasses, emerging from their pots like miniature volcanoes.

mouthful for a fabulous little **Japanese maple**, growing infinitely slowly to 1.2m/4ft. It forms a spreading mound of fingered, finely cut, bronze-red leaves which sigh in every breath of wind. The autumn colour is good, too, and even in winter the elegantly curved branches are extremely attractive. But just a tip – they cost an arm and a leg, so be sure to provide the rich compost (John Innes No 2 or No 3) and partial shade that they prefer; blazing sun can scorch the delicate leaves.

Sticking with the oriental look, how about **bamboos**? The individual leaves aren't tremendously exciting, but the overall effect is of an arching waterfall of green. Those with white variegation have an especially light touch and white-striped *Arundinaria variegata* (now *Pleioblastus variegatus*) grows to a moderate – in bamboo terms – 1.2m/4ft. Lovely in sun or part shade, so long as you keep the compost moist.

Like bamboos, the **ornamental grasses**, for so long neglected, are now back in favour. There's an enormous range, but do look out for *Hakonechloa macra* 'Aureola' – shaggy-headed clumps to 40cm/16in tall, maturing from yellow and green striped to a warm red-brown. And for the black grass, *Ophiopogon planiscapus* 'Nigrescens' – a tiny 15cm/6in plant with strappy, curved leaves that are truly black. It can get lost in a garden planting, but looks terrific in pots and will slowly spread into a small clump.

By way of complete contrast, take a look at those old faithfuls for pots, the handsome hostas. These are solid, robust plants, forming dense rosettes of ribbed leaves. One of the most widely available, *Hosta crispula*, has lance-shaped leaves with an irregular white edging which is perfect for lighting up a shady spot. Even bolder is the remarkable *Hosta sieboldiana elegans* which produces enormous 30cm/12in wide, corrugated leaves in a beautiful blue-grey – rather like a piece of living sculpture.

SHAPING UP

Clipped box (*Buxus*) is a wonderful addition to any part of the garden, whether to stand sentinel in pairs by a doorway, or to mark the corners of a vegetable bed. Spirals are wonderfully ornamental, but by far the easiest to maintain are the box balls – lovely little green potted puddings that look good even in the worst winter weather. And if you do forget to clip them over in spring, you can simply explain that you're training them into hedgehogs.

Boxing clever – a mature spiral and a collection of younger pre-shaped box balls.

The combination of glossy evergreen leaves and exotic blooms (here, 'Adolphe Audusson') makes camellia one of the most desirable of permanent pot plants.

PERENNIAL EYE-CATCHERS

While bedding plants supply most of the summer colour in pots and tubs, don't forget that there are other, permanent, plants that will provide colourful displays year after year.

Start the season off with a bang with camellias. With their large, exotic blooms and dense, glossy foliage, they make an excellent backdrop for summer bedding displays. They can, in fact, be in flower as early as November, with some varieties still blooming in May. Three of the loveliest are the stunning silver-pink 'Donation', rich pink, peony-flowered 'Anticipation', and 'Adolphe Audusson', with enormous scarlet blooms that can be as much as 13cm/5in across. All camellias are best in a west- or sheltered north-facing position, in partial shade, planted in ericaceous compost.

To bridge the gap between spring and summer, invest in a few dwarf rhododendrons or azaleas, most of which, like camellias, are evergreen. The colour range is incredible, so your April/May potted garden can be as quiet (soft pinks and whites) or as loud (screaming reds, bellowing yellows) as you like.

When summer does finally arrive, it's roses that will provide displays to rival the flower-power of your

The smaller, prostrate forms of ceanothus grow well in a large pot and can be lightly trimmed to keep them in good shape.

bedding plants. And with miniature or patio roses (30-45cm/12-18in), it seems a positive kindness to grow them in pots. Out in the garden, they're easily overlooked (or swamped by other plants) but potted up, their miniature charms can be highlighted and enjoyed closer to eye-level.

The more compact forms of groundcover roses are eminently suitable too, as are the smaller hybrid teas and floribundas, and will give lashings of colour. And have a look at the English roses, bred by David Austin. They're an informal, bushy shape, with gorgeous, very fully-petalled flowers and fantastic scents, from classic tea rose through fruity tones to myrrh-like fragrances. There are several fairly short varieties and 'The Prince', at 60cm/2ft, is quite magnificent – cupped rosettes of deep crimson maturing to rich royal purple, with an equally rich fragrance.

Making the most of
Spring Bulbs

By early March, after the dank days of January and February when time and the garden seem to stand still, gardeners throughout the land are to be seen pacing and fretting, poking hopefully at clumps of bright leaves, checking the sky for any hint of sun that will spur their plants on.

It's an anxious wait, those tantalising days when the daffodils seem to hang around in bud forever. And it is such a joy when they do finally come trumpeting through, to give the first real splash of colour of the year, closely followed by the tulips that will keep your pots and tubs in good cheer right through to May.

GOLDEN WONDERS

The great thing about daffodils is that they're the best of all bulbs for permanent residence in larger pots and tubs. Add them to perennial container plants (as an

Double up on flower power by planting bulbs in layers – the result, as this terracotta bowl of 'Geranium' daffodils demonstrates, can be quite spectacular.

POTTED SPRING SUNSHINE

Golden crocus stretch out their petals to drink in every drop of sun in this beautiful spring planting in a 30cm/12in half-pot. Just one plant of the prostrate heather, *Erica carnea* 'Springwood Pink', is enough here, the pink trails picking their way delicately between the crocuses.

INGREDIENTS
• 20 x *Crocus*, gold
• 1 x dwarf fir *(Abies)*
• 2 x *Erica carnea* 'Springwood Pink'

❀ *Dainty species crocus like golden 'E.P. Bowles' are lovely for an early (February) scheme, the larger-flowered Dutch crocus for April colour.*

❀ *Erica carnea 'Springwood White' has the same ground-hugging habit as 'Springwood Pink' and would look equally good.*

HIGH WATTAGE BULBS

To get maximum pleasure from your spring bulbs, plant them so that each variety can be displayed to its very best advantage. An explosive mix of variously coloured tulips, daffodils and hyacinths, or an assortment of daffodils that you've picked from the cram-a-bag selection at the garden centre, will give you a colourful show at close quarters, certainly. But when you view it from any distance, each individual bulb will have lost its identity, its character; like a roomful of babbling people, it's hard to pick out particular voices.

So separate them out into coherent groups – have a pot of one variety of daffodil next to a pot of another, rather than mixing the two; a pot planted up with one type of dwarf kaufmanniana or greigii tulip, so that you can really appreciate the sturdy little flowers and the maroon-striped leaves.

In tubs, plant them in clumps, the way their ancestors grew in the wild, rather than dotting them about. By all means grow different varieties in the same tub, but give each one room to shine. Bulbs are talented plants and, while they're good in the chorus line, they're just brilliant in the spotlight.

Large tubs of tall 'Rembrandt' tulips set off low pots of 'Dove White' narcissus, pansies and violas.

annual golden frill for a narrow conifer for instance), or use them as part of a bedding scheme in spring and simply cut back the dying leaves and plant summer bedding over them when May comes round. The other good trick is to double up on flower power by planting in layers   the top layer at the normal depth, with a second layer 5cm/2in or so deeper. Despite the slight depth difference, they'll all flower at the same time for a double-density display. And dainty varieties like 'Tete-a-Tete' look superb planted up in a wicker basket with a pale yellow primrose or two, topped off with moss and placed on a garden table.

Daffodils don't have to be gold, of course; they can be all shades from best butter to lemon, cream and ice white, with trumpets that can vary from red-rimmed to deepest orange. So take your pick – the only line we, personally, draw is when it comes to pink-tinted varieties. The great delight of early spring colour is its clarity, its freshness; pink just doesn't fill the bill.

Come to think of it, there's another line we draw. The beauty of daffodils is their poise and the clean lines and simplicity of the flowers, from the bold gold classic shape of 'Fortune' to the long, narrow trumpets and swept-back petals of a little gem like

The shaggy golden heads of little 'Rip van Winkle' contrast well with the bright blue daisy flowers of Anemone blanda.

'Jumblie'. So we're not too fond of those doubles which can look heavy and clumsy next to their more natural cousins or where the grace of the flower is sacrificed at the altar of novelty.

A TOUCH OF THE BLUES

Golds and whites predominate in early spring, with a swelling chorus of warmer, more vivid colour from tulips as the season progresses. And there isn't one single daffodil or tulip that won't look even more handsome with an underplanting of that other great spring colour, blue.

The delightful little (30cm/12in) narcissus 'February Gold' is optimistically named, since it normally flowers in March, and there are several dainty blues that would set it off to perfection. *Puschkinia libanotica*, the striped squill, produces 10cm/4in heads of pale silvery blue bells, while the similar *Scilla siberica* has bells of a deeper, more royal blue. *Anemone blanda* is another good blue for larger pots and tubs, forming a low mat of finely cut leaves studded with large daisy flowers.

A powerful combination of fragrances from hyacinths, wall-flowers and the most beautiful late-flowering daffodil, 'Actaea'.

For April/May flower, there's one blue beauty that has been sadly neglected and deserves to be much more widely grown. It's called *Ipheion*, and the blue form is the lovely 'Wisley Blue' with wide, mauve-blue flowers to 12.5cm/5in, with a sweetly honeyed scent. It's lovely in sun or partial shade, in a well-drained soil.

All bulbs so far, but we haven't forgotten the forget-me-not *(Myosotis)* – a haze of piercing blue flowers that look wonderful with the last bright spring tulips. And if you shake a flowered plant over a spare piece of ground, you'll have a colony of seedlings, free, for next year's displays. Winter pansies are invaluable too, in all shades from palest to deepest blue; those with black 'faces' are especially characterful.

THE FINAL FLING

It's the compact varieties of tulip that are so useful and so widely grown in pots and tubs, and certainly they're the ones we recommend as most appropriate. But could we urge you to break the rules just for once and try some really tall ones as well? There are some truly spectacular May-flowering varieties – the lily-flowered, the viridiflora, the fringed and the parrot tulips – that are so fancy and fantastical they have to be included.

Most of them grow to around 60cm/2ft, so you'll need a large pot or tub to accommodate them – and a sheltered position where the wind won't knock them about. And if you have trouble finding a good

One of the freshest, coolest colour combinations of all – the delicate green striping and shading of viridiflora tulip 'Spring Green'.

INSTANT SPRING IMPACT

For a ready-made display, take advantage of the potted spring bulbs at your local garden centre – then cheat a little. It's very fashionable to use cut flowers in planted containers and here a vase has been sunk into a 40cm/16in pot to accommodate some florist's irises. Give it a try - no one will know!

INGREDIENTS
- 3 x bunches Dutch iris
- 4 x *Narcissus* 'Rembrandt'
- 3 x *Tulipa* 'Monte Carlo'
- 10 x *Muscari*
- 3 x *Anemone de Caen*, blue
- 2 x *Viola*

selection at your garden centre, just send off for a mail order catalogue from one of the many bulb specialists who advertise in gardening magazines and you'll be spoiled for choice.

The lily-flowered tulips are quite extraordinary. Their tall, wiry stems carry blooms which, instead of tapering to a point, send the tips of the petals flaring out in elongated curves. The effect is immensely light and elegant, almost as if the flowers were dancing. One of the loveliest is the aptly-named 'Ballerina', a soft glowing orange and, rare for the tulip tribe, it's scented. 'Ballade' is another beauty, each magenta petal boldly outlined in white.

Viridiflora tulips are another intriguing group, with a bold stripe of green up the centre of each lightly waved petal. The effect is at its freshest in the white-based 'Spring Green', and at its most dramatic in deep rose-pink 'Esperanto', its eye-catching qualities further enhanced by white-banded leaves.

Flower arrangers love the fringed tulips. They're the classic tulip egg shape, but the tip of each petal is covered in a very fine, delicate fringe that looks almost like ice crystals. Primrose yellow 'Maja' and deep pink 'Burgundy Lacce' are exceptionally pretty.

Saving the best of them for last, have you ever been squawked at by a parrot tulip? It's an astounding experience. Their huge flowers, up to 20cm/8in across, are outrageously feathered and frilled. Deep purple

For your delight – 'Heart's Delight' is an early-flowering kaufmanniana tulip with the distinctive maroon leaf-striping.

'Black Parrot' is amazing enough, but some of the multicoloured varieties will really knock you off your perch. 'Estella Rijnveld' is particularly riotous, looking like something a confectioner whipped up using ice cream and raspberry sauce. Quite delicious.

Making the most of Shady Spots

Shade comes in all shades, from lightest to darkest, but there's no reason for any shady spot to be without a full furnishing of plants. The commonest source of shade (woodland gardens apart) is buildings – and the likelihood is that the area around the building is paved. Which makes pots and tubs absolutely invaluable for turning a dank, gloomy corner into something more akin to a secret glade, and a relatively open, north-facing spot into a jungle of foliage and flowers.

So grab all the containers you can find, fill them up with plants from the huge range that are shade-tolerant and sit back and admire your handiwork.

LIGHTING UP TIME

Even really gloomy areas – tiny basements for instance, or the dark corner at the angle of two buildings where the focal feature is usually a dustbin – can be clothed with plants. Admittedly the choice is limited, but you can turn this into an asset by creating a cool, leafy (and mostly green) retreat with tons of atmosphere.

Deck the walls with ivy (dark green *Hedera hibernica* is good), plant a *Fatsia japonica* in a tub, for its huge jungly leaves, add one of the spotted laurels (*Aucuba japonica*) for a touch of gold, and compact *Prunus laurocerasus* 'Otto Luyken' for its glossy, light-catching leaves and white flowers. Fill in around this main structure with smaller evergreens like ferns (any of the *Dryopteris* will do well), miniature box (*Buxus sempervirens* 'Suffruticosa'), hostas, lamiums and *Euphorbia robbiae*. And to enliven this evergreen grotto in summer, set out a few pots of colourful busy lizzies (*Impatiens*), which will thrive here.

Fatsia japonica is one of the noblest of all evergreens for shade, with enormous, tropical leaves. Prune in April if you need to control the height and the spread.

How to furnish a shady spot with style:
(above) a bracken-lined basket houses a pretty
collection of ferns
(right) the airy, delicate fronds of ferns are used to
highlight the solidity of the fat, ribbed leaves of
mixed hostas in a grouping around the front door.

That's just a taste of the splendid picture you can create in a seemingly impossible spot. Nab the expert at your local garden centre and he or she will be happy to introduce you to a whole host more shade-tolerant plants.

When it comes to partially shaded positions – a north wall that's not directly overlooked by other walls or buildings, for instance, or the dappled shade cast by a tree, you'll find a splendid range of plants that will flourish. Any amount of foliage plants will love it – in fact all you have to do is dispense with the real sun lovers and take your pick.

You'll have a bit more trouble finding perennial flowering plants to fit the partial shade bill, but spring bulbs will happily cope, and can light up the whole area from February right through to May. And in early summer, rhododendrons and azaleas will put on a terrific display and look even better here than in full sun.

For later colour, two prolific climbing roses will do well in tubs – 'Golden Showers' and 'Paul's Scarlet Climber' are both shade-tolerant, growing to little more than 3m/10ft. Many clematis, too, flower well in shade. Deep purple 'The President' and shell-pink 'Hagley Hybrid', for instance, can be planted to twine affectionately through the roses – the contrast between opulent rose and simple starry clematis is lovely.

But it's bedding plants that come to your rescue if you want really colourful, long-lasting summer displays in partial shade. So cram in the busy lizzies and begonias in all their bright colours; the large-flowered tuberous begonias, in particular, are exceptionally luminous. Bright mimulus (monkey musk) will love it so long as it's kept well watered. Sweet-scented nicotianas (tobacco plants) will be happy here too, and the salmon-pink form of the popular 'Domino' series really shines out. And plug any gaps with the best of all shade-loving bedding plants, the fuchsia; the choice of colour and form is vast, but our all-time favourites are the romantic 'Annabel' – fully double, in creamy white tinged with pink – and the jolly 'Swingtime' – costumed in red with voluminous white skirts. They'll grow in sun, too, but in shade they'll really have a ball.

SHADY SPOTS

The pink mopheads of Hydrangea *'Altona' will light up this shady corner of a garden for months on end.*

HAPPY HYDRANGEAS

Hydrangeas? Those miserable things that sit looking dry, dusty and dull in front gardens? That's the usual reaction to any suggestion of planting hydrangeas. And it's this sunny front garden situation that has given them such a bad name. Because the poor things are baking, and gasping for the regular water that's essential to their wellbeing.

Put them in a shady, but not too gloomy, spot, keep them well watered, and they're a different beast altogether – lush, vibrant, bouncing with health and happiness and brimming with beautiful flowers.

The mophead types are the best known – great globes of flower from July right through to September – and one of the neatest for tubs is 'Preziosa' (90cm/3ft) with rosy pink-red mops and deep green leaves that mature to bronze-purple. Even prettier, we think, and with a more delicate touch, are the lacecap varieties, with a ring of large flowers around a central circle of tiny florets. 'Bluebird' is one of the most compact (90cm/3ft) and exceedingly pretty. Leave the flowerheads on over winter, to provide a little frost protection for the developing buds, and just pinch them off in spring.

And just a tip: most hydrangeas are perfectly happy in John Innes No 3 compost, but the blues are tricker. The lime in the soil will turn them to sludgy pink. So apply a blueing compound, available at garden centres, or grow them in ericaceous compost.

BRIGHT COLOUR FOR A SHADY SPOT

The perfect planting for partial shade, in rich magenta-purple and piercing pink. Nicotianas and busy lizzies (*Impatiens*) thrive in shade and the petunias, although best in a sunny position, will cope remarkably well in an open, north facing one in this 45cm/18in pot.

INGREDIENTS
• 4 x *Nicotiana* 'Domino Salmon Pink'
• 6 x *Impatiens* 'Accent Mixed'
• 1 x *Gypsophila* 'Festival White'
• 1 x *Petunia* 'Surfinia Purple'

❀ *Surfinia petunias are very vigorous and will form a pool of purple around the pot, but don't be afraid to chop them back if need be.*

Making the most of Scent

Some scents will swamp you with their lushness, others tickle your nose with their freshness, some will be so elusive that you'll spend hours tracking them down, some don't happen until evening, some don't happen at all unless you crush the plant. And some have the most unlikely origin – the sticky moss-like growth on moss roses, for instance, is richly spicy.

With one of the richest of all spring scents, hyacinths look particularly effective in single-colour groups.

The one thing all these scents have in common is that they're essential ingredients for all-round enjoyment of the garden. So plan for colour and texture to your heart's content, but don't neglect to follow your nose and plan for plenty of scent too.

Place a pot of camomile close to your favourite seat, grow sweet peas in tubs, tobacco plants (*Nicotiana*) in pots close to the house so that the fragrance can waft indoors, make sure when buying petunias that you include a few purples for their opulent perfume. Plant plenty of lilies and scented varieties of daffodil. Indulge yourself.

LUSCIOUS LILIES

People sometimes shy away from growing lilies because their exotic looks somehow suggest that they could be difficult to please. Nothing could be further from the truth, and they're ideal for pots – just wheel them into pride of place as the first buds break and you can spend long happy summer evenings enjoying the splendiferous flowers and drinking in the lush perfumes.

But choose with care. Despite their marvellous reputation for scent, some varieties, while they are beautiful and well

Grow sweet peas in a large pot on a wigwam of bamboo canes and relish their sweet, peppery fragrance.

worth growing, have none at all. Our first choice for scent would always be *Lilium regale*, growing to 1.2m/4ft. The large waxy trumpets are pure white within and tenderly striped with pale pink-purple on the outside and the combination of the powerful fragrance (which lingers all around) with the sweet simplicity and purity of the flowers is irresistible.

Bulb expert, grower and Chelsea gold medal winner, John Amand, agrees with us about the richness of *Lilium regale*'s scent, and suggests five more all-time favourites for fragrance:

Lilium *'Star Gazer'*

Lilium *'Casa Blanca'*

'Casa Blanca': Extra-large starry flowers of pure white, set off by deep orange stamens. 90cm/3ft.

'Golden Splendour': Deep orange/yellow trumpets with a maroon striping on the reverse. 1.2m/4ft.

***Lilium longiflorum*:** Exceptionally long (to 20cm/8in) white trumpets. Overwinter indoors. To 90cm/3ft.

'Pink Perfection': Large trumpets suffused with shades of palest to deep rose pink. 1.2m/4ft.

'Star Gazer': Stunning open trumpets of crimson-pink spotted with maroon and edged in white. 90cm/3ft.

SCENTED DAFFODILS

All daffodils, whether classified as scented or not, have a unique aroma. Light, clean and fresh, rather like the invigorating waft of air that accompanies someone returning from a brisk walk on a frosty day. It's a delicate scent, but on a warm spring day, especially in a small, sheltered garden, it's delicious.

But there are certainly plenty of daffodils with a more positive scent, and the shorter varieties are excellent candidates for the potted garden. One of the

STOCKING UP ON SCENT

The spicy clove scent of stocks is one of the great pleasures of mid-summer and here their fat spikes of pink and white double flowers contrast beautifully with the ruff of simple violas at their base, in a sturdy 35cm/14in pot.

INGREDIENTS
• 9 x *Matthiola* (Brompton stocks)
• 10 x *Viola* (purple selection)

❀ *This pot will perform well in sun or partial shade – place it close to a favourite seat so that you can really savour the rich perfume of the stocks.*

SCENTED-LEAF GERANIUMS

If you're lucky enough to have a garden centre that stocks scented-leaf geraniums, snap them up immediately and cram them into pots and tubs. They really are quite brilliant plants – tough, trouble-free, and growing at a tremendous rate in the freedom of a large pot, even in shady spots. Place them where you'll brush past and release the strongly aromatic fragrances.

You're probably already familiar with the lemon-scented types that used to be in the window of every Greek café in the land – but there's a whole world of other scents to be savoured: *Pelargonium odoratissimum*, with tiny felted leaves smelling of fresh green apples, *Pelargonium tomentosum*, a vigorous peppermint-scented trailer with enormous velvety leaves; *Pelargonium fragrans* and 'Creamy Nutmeg' for pine scents; 'Clorinda' for cedar; 'Attar of Roses' for – yes, you're right – a rose aroma.

They're every bit as easy to overwinter as the geraniums we grow for their flowers (see p. 54) and, what's more, a couple of lemon- or rose-scented leaves will liven up an apple pie no end.

A lemon-scented aristocat, 'Lady Plymouth', with cream-edged cut leaves and pretty pink flowers.

PLANTING FOR SCENT

littler fish in the perfumed pond is 'Minnow', a multi-headed marvel at 15cm/6in, with rounded, creamy yellow petals and a lemon cup. 'Baby Moon' (20cm/8in) is even more exquisite – fine reed-like leaves, with several miniature golden flowers to a stem and a piercing, lemony scent. Plant them in generous clumps in terracotta pots, add in a few *Scilla siberica* for their dangling blue heads, and you'll have an instant spring garden in miniature.

For slightly larger pots and tubs, try two white daffodils that are right at the top of our shopping list. Sweetly scented 'Thalia' has a poise and grace that will take your breath away – milky white flowers with swept-back petals, hovering in twos and threes on 30cm/12in stems. The 'pheasant's eye' narcissus 'Actaea' is somewhat taller at 40cm/16in, but utterly beautiful for a spot that's sheltered from wind. It has glistening white petals round a tiny red-rimmed eye, and a scent that's almost as rich as a lily. They're both so lovely that it pays to highlight them against a plain background – in a tub with a sheet of dark green ivy as a backcloth, or planted densely in a circle around a deep green, upright-growing conifer.

Narcissus poeticus *'Actaea'*

Making the most of
Gardens in Miniature

We once ran a 'Garden in a Seed Tray' competition in conjunction with a children's television programme and the response was just amazing. We were swamped by beautifully crafted little gardens with mirrors for lakes, sand for paths, gravel for rocks, pebbles for mountains and snippings of shrubs for trees. So if you're still a child at heart, have a go at creating a miniature landscape in a sink or trough – the effect can be quite exquisite.

GETTING GOING

Your first requirement is a flat-bottomed sink or trough that looks reasonably rustic. Old stone sinks cost a fortune, but second-hand white ceramic sinks are cheaper and it's easy to give them an instant stone look.

CHOOSING THE PLANTS

The best plants for miniature garden are alpines and small succulents, such as stonecrop, which all need sharp drainage. You'll find plenty of recommendations in Best Rockery Plants (see p. 94) but basically what you're looking for are those that stay neat and compact.

CREATING A STONE-LOOK SINK

1. Thoroughly clean the sink to remove any greasy soap deposits, then score the surface and apply contact adhesive to the outer walls, rim and top 5cm/2in of the inner walls.
2. Mix together 1 part cement, 2 parts coarse sand and 2 parts peat substitute such as coir compost. Add water until you have a thick, stiff paste.

3. Using a trowel, apply a 13mm/$\frac{1}{2}$in coating of the mix to the sink, keeping it even and firming it down. Round off the edges using gloved hands.
4. After a week or so, roughen up the surface with a wire brush to make it look even more natural, and coat with liquid manure to encourage mosses and lichens to grow.

A miniature landscape packed with exquisite treasures, set against mossy rocks. It is easy to maintain, too, since most alpines and dwarf conifers are very slow growing.

More vigorous, spreading plants will soon look out of proportion, and need constant cutting back or lifting and dividing. So steer clear of rampers like arabis, aubrieta and *Saxifraga umbrosa* (London pride), which look fine on a rockery but can be overwhelming in a miniature landscape. Substitute the ground-eating *Cerastium tomentosum* (grey leaved, white-flowered snow-in-summer) by the much better-mannered *C. alpinum*.

5. To provide the sharp drainage required by most alpines and succulents, cover the bottom of the sink with a 5cm/2in layer of coarse gravel, broken pots or garden stones to prevent compost from blocking the drainage hole. Standing the sink on pot feet or bricks will also help drainage.

6. Fill the sink garden up with a mix of 3 parts John Innes No 2 compost, 1 part fine grit, to within 2.5cm/1in of the rim, firming as you go. You are then ready to put in your selected plants.

MINIATURE WATER GARDENS

A pond or pool is a lovely garden feature, but it is not always possible where space is at a premium. So compromise by creating a tiny water garden in a container. On the very smallest scale, even a wide-mouthed urn (without drainage holes, of course) can be filled with water, so that the surface glimmers and reflects the sun and sky – very simple, and very pleasing.

For something more sophisticated, line a half-barrel with butyl or heavy-duty polythene and fill with water. You can then add a few oxygenating plants – parrot's feather *(Miriophyllum aquaticum)* sends up lovely fine-feathered fronds above the water – and a couple of diminutive water plants like the dainty bulrush *Typha minima* and the small but perfectly formed white water lily *Nymphaea* 'Pygmaea Alba'. Even without fish (in a barrel they'll fry in summer and freeze in winter), your miniature pond will be a source of great pleasure.

A sink or trough filled with neat plants is very pretty, but to give it scale and the feel of a genuine, though tiny, landscape, you also need rocks and trees. Place the rocks (many larger garden centres stock cobbles and various types of ornamental stone) close to a little group of plants, so that they nestle against them as they would in the wild. And stick to one kind of rock, so that it looks like a natural outcrop rather than a geology lesson.

ADDING HEIGHT

For your trees, choose from the slowest growing of the dwarf conifers. They can be bought at a few inches tall, and it will be many years before they reach a height that's out of scale with a sink garden. There's a lovely little spruce, *Picea abies* 'Gregoryana', that makes a billowing dome of sea-green and grows at a snail's pace. The cypress family *(Chamaecyparis)* contains many attractive dwarf forms that will creep up by less than 2.5cm/1in a year – silver-tipped glaucous 'Pygmaea Argentea' is a gem. And *Abies balsamea hudsonia* is one of the best of the dwarf silver firs, making a rounded bush of densely packed deep green needles.

When your planting is complete, finish off with a 2.5cm/1in layer of gravel. This not only looks good, but prevents too much moisture from lingering around the crown (the point from which top growth starts) of the plants.

Hanging Baskets

There's something very special about hanging baskets. Because the impact they create, and the pleasure they give, is totally out of proportion to their size. Just one basket, flowering away all summer, can totally transform the drabbest area. It's a magical effect and the real beauty of it is that anyone who's prepared to take a little extra time and trouble can achieve wonderful results.

Use hanging baskets anywhere – by the front door, along the side of the house, or to add extra colour to a pergola. In summer, cram them with a profusion of bedding plants, or do a bit of high-rise farming by using them to grow tomatoes, strawberries or herbs. And don't pack them away in autumn. Give them a new lease of life with winter-flowering pansies, heathers, colourful evergreens and spring bulbs.

They're not, admittedly, as easy to look after as pots, tubs and window boxes, especially in summer. But it's great fun to pull out all the stops, just for once, and create something totally stunning.

Even the simplest hanging basket, like this bright mix of busy lizzies, can bring months of good cheer.

CHOOSING A BASKET
WIRE BASKETS

The traditional wire basket is the most popular of all because you can plant up the sides as well as the top, to create a tumbling mass of colour. They're made from plastic-coated wire and should last for years. But just a tip – go for the more discreet green or black models; the white ones stick out like a sore thumb until the plants have grown sufficiently to disguise them.

Sizes generally range from 25cm/10in to 40cm/16in in diameter, and the size you choose makes quite a difference to the results you can achieve and to the amount of watering that will be needed. The smallest baskets hold fewer plants, so they make a less impressive display and, even worse, will dry out faster because they hold less compost. And at the other end of the scale, the

40cm/16in baskets have their problems. They make spectacular displays, and they need less frequent watering because they hold so much compost, but they're fearsomely heavy, especially when they've just been watered. So make sure that they're on extra-strong brackets and be prepared for some back-breaking work when you're moving them.

Of the two in-between sizes, our vote would always be for the 35cm/14in baskets which, surprisingly, hold 50 per cent more compost than the 30cm/12in. So watering isn't too much of a chore, they're a manageable size, and you can create some excellent displays: the best of all possible worlds.

Wire baskets do need to be lined, of course, to keep the compost in, and by far the most natural effect is

CHOOSING A BASKET

achieved by moss. The easiest to use is sphagnum moss but as it comes from peat bogs, 'green' gardeners might prefer the more threadlike moss that's gathered from conifer plantations. Whichever you choose, moss-lined baskets do need the most frequent watering.

Other types of liner are better at water retention. Coco-fibre matting looks reasonably natural, can be cut to size, helps insulate roots and can be used a second year; but, although there are slits for side-planting, they do rather limit the number of plants you can use as it's virtually impossible to cut through to make more holes. Wool mats are similarly unyielding. Foam liners are cheap and a bit too cheerful; avoid the multicoloured versions like the plague – they'll give you a headache. And rigid fibre liners are, we think, pretty useless because, again, making holes for side planting is incredibly difficult. Use black polythene instead – it's just as ugly but at least it's cheaper. All in all, as you may have gathered, when it comes to lining baskets, we much prefer moss!

A final piece of advice: wire baskets aren't for the fainthearted. They're fiddly to plant up and watering them can be a real chore in hot weather. But if you want a truly magnificent display, nothing can beat them.

BRACKETS FOR BASKETS

Hanging basket brackets are sold in a range of sizes to suit different diameter baskets, so make sure the arm is long enough to hold the planted basket well clear of the wall. Some of the more sophisticated models have swivels which enable you to turn the basket occasionally, for even growth. Others have pulleys or spring-loaded holders which make watering far easier – you just lower the basket to waist height, water, then send it sailing back up. But whichever you buy, make sure they're fixed very firmly to the wall. A well watered basket can weigh 11kg/25lb or more, so don't take any chances – fix them properly.

PLASTIC BASKETS

Plastic baskets are really hanging pots, and they have a number of advantages over wire baskets. No liner is needed and planting is far simpler (you only have to worry about what goes in the top). Watering is easier too because there's no evaporation from the sides, and most models have a clip-on drip tray which acts as a mini-reservoir. They're great value for money, but they'll never be as full and lush as a wire basket, and they can look rather stark until the trailing plants have bushed out to disguise them.

SELF-WATERING BASKETS

Self-watering baskets really do make life easier. A reservoir is concealed within the base, separated from the compost by capillary matting. Water seeps up continually through the matting so that the compost is kept constantly moist. All you need to do is top up the reservoir every week or so. Again, they can only be planted at the top and they do need trailers to soften their appearance, but for busy (or just forgetful) gardeners they're a great boon.

This close-mesh wire basket houses a delightfully simple planting for late spring, using the variegated ivy, Hedera helix *'Glacier', and the piercing blue flowers of forget-me-nots (*Myosotis*), which bloom from April through to June.*

Wall-mounted Babyllon bowls give a fully rounded globe of colour and are both quick and easy to plant up.

BABYLLON BOWLS

These bowl-shaped planters are made from a circle of wide, curved finger-like prongs, mounted on to a special wall bracket. They can be planted from top to bottom for really full displays. Since there are no chains, they don't swing round in the wind but they can be rotated for even growth. But they are more expensive than conventional baskets and, because the prongs are widely spaced, it's a good idea to use more mature (and therefore pricier) bedding plants (those that are bought in 9cm/3½in pots) when planting up.

FLOWER POUCHES AND FLOWER TOWERS

These are simple flexible plastic tubes that are filled with compost, planted at the marked positions, then hung up (see the photograph on p. 57). They can look magnificent as long as the entire tube is kept evenly watered, so that the plants at the bottom get as much water as those at the top. Some are sold with built-in water reservoirs, others with water-retention gels. For balanced growth, it's also important that each plant gets its fair share of food – but if you've got the watering right, the feeding should be fine too.

TIPS

✔ *Unfortunately – and we speak from experience here – beautifully planted baskets are quite a temptation for opportunist thieves. To deter them, padlock your basket to the bracket, or buy one of the baskets that are now available with built-in security devices.*

✔ *Although wire hanging baskets should last for years, their chains may not. So check them thoroughly before you hang the basket up. Replacement chains can be bought from most garden centres.*

✔ *If you're using plastic baskets in winter, remove the drip tray as it can lead to waterlogging of the compost and rotting of the plants. Similarly, self-watering baskets can stay just too wet in winter, so they are best used for summer displays only.*

✔ *Have a go at making your own basket. We've seen some superb planters made from inverted lampshade frames lined with wide-mesh chicken wire then mossed, planted and hung up. But do check that the original joints are firmly soldered before using one.*

Growing Success

The very best hanging baskets are those where the basket itself disappears, overwhelmed by a massive explosion of leaves and flowers. Pubs and restaurants, in particular, specialize in spectacular displays and, while these baskets are usually planted up by professionals, you can achieve just the same effect at home. All it takes for a really successful basket that will stay looking wonderful right through summer are the three P's – Planning, Planting and Pampering. Here's how .....

Make the most of your hanging basket by choosing plants that echo the colour of surrounding plantings.

PLANNING

Once you've accumulated the hardware (basket, liner, bracket etc), make sure you choose a **good compost.** Special hanging basket compost is available, which is specially formulated to help retain moisture, but a good quality multi-purpose compost will do much the same job slightly more cheaply. Avoid heavier loam-based John Innes composts – you'll end up with a weighty basket that could put a strain on the bracket, and on your back.

Then comes the interesting bit – your **selection of plants.** Young plants are the best for planting the sides of wire baskets, because they're easy to winkle through the wire. More established plants can be used for top plantings, depending on your budget.

Pick out the sturdiest, bushiest plants. The ones to avoid are those with any sign of disease or yellowing, any that have become drawn and spindly, any that feel very light when you pick them up (they've been allowed to dry out) and any with a mass of roots emerging from the base of the pot or strip (they've used up all the nutrients in the compost and are quietly starving).

In this cheerful globe of colour brightening an entrance, the basket itself is totally obscured by the billowing planting of begonias, bidens, lobelia, petunias, busy lizzies, fuchsia and helichrysum.

PLANTING

Whatever type of basket you're planting up, always water the plants well beforehand. This helps to keep the rootball intact, and makes it very much easier to deal with plants in strips – root damage is inevitable when splitting them up, but a moist soil allows you to do a certain amount of teasing, rather than tearing, apart.

Planting a mossed wire basket

As we've already said, we're not great fans of basket liners, much preferring the more natural look of moss, but by all means substitute a liner for moss in the following planting recipe.

• Set the basket on a bowl or bucket to keep it steady and line the base with moss, firming it down so that there's a good thick layer that won't leak compost. Place a plastic saucer or a piece of polythene over this, to help retain water. Top up with compost to the level of the moss.

GROWING SUCCESS

1 *Line the basket thickly with moss or an alternative (here, a moss substitute made from coir fibre).*

2 *Set a circle of primulas (*Primula *'Wanda') close to the rim and place trailing ivy in the top of the basket.*

3 *Fill in with compost, firming it down with your hands and taking care not to leave any gaps.*

4 *Top the basket with the pompon flowers of bellis daisies and with ranunculus. Water well and hang it where the delicious mix of pinks will give maximum enjoyment.*

• Set in your first circle of plants (bush lobelia for instance) close to the base, 7.5cm/3in apart. Push them through from the outside, being as gentle as possible with the roots, so that the rootball is resting on the compost.

• Top up with more moss and compost and add a second circle of plants, positioned so that they don't directly overhang those below them. Carry on in this way until you reach the top of the basket. Larger baskets will happily accommodate three circles of plants, and will guarantee a wonderfully full, lush planting.

• Finally, plant up the top of the basket. In a mixed basket, use a dominant plant as a centrepiece – an upright geranium, for instance – and fill in with smaller plants and a few trailers. Fill in any gaps with more compost, and top up any sunken areas which may appear after you've given the basket a thorough watering.

Planting other types of basket

Planting up a **plastic basket** is just like planting up an ordinary pot (see p. 14), but we do like to use a good proportion of vigorous trailers round the side so that when they're fully grown, the plastic does a vanishing act.

Flower pouches and **towers** are equally easy – just fill them up with compost and make planting holes by slitting the plastic where indicated, or plant in pre-cut holes.

Planting **Babyllon bowls** is a bit like building a wall, and more mature plants, with well established rootballs, are the easiest to handle when planting one up. Set in the liner supplied, then place the first layer of plants between the curved 'fingers' of the bowl. Fill in the gaps between the rootballs with tightly rolled moss. Then build up a second layer by placing moss above rootball, rootball above moss. Carry on until you reach the top of the basket, fill the centre of the bowl with compost and plant the top.

PAMPERING
Watering

Plants like to grow smoothly and evenly, so watering is a critical factor. Mossed baskets are the most vulnerable to drying out and in very hot weather can need watering twice a day, so check them regularly and try to water in the cool of the morning or evening, when less moisture will be lost by evaporation. Mixing water crystals with the compost when planting up helps too – they swell up into water-retaining globules which act as little reservoirs. If a mossed basket dries out completely, re-wet it by plunging it in a deep bowl for an hour or so.

And how to water easily when baskets are well above head height? A Hi-Lo pulley will enable you to lower the plant to your level, or you can buy long, specially angled hose-lances to do the stretching for you. If you have lots of baskets to look after, you could invest in an irrigation system. But if you're quite happy using steps to reach your baskets, do make sure they're steady, and water from a 1-litre plastic bottle, to save having to lift a heavy watering can.

TIPS

✔ *If one plant in a mixed planting grows rather too enthusiastically, don't be afraid to cut it back. Similarly, if plants become leggy (pansies and petunias, in particular, flower on ever-elongating stems), chop them back – you'll lose a bit of colour for a while, but they'll soon bounce back.*

✔ *Summer bedding baskets should never be set outdoors while there's still any danger of frost, but if you've a light, frost-free room such as a porch or conservatory, it certainly pays to plant them up early and grow them on, so that you'll have something pretty substantial to hang out by late May or early June.*

✔ *Make a fantastic globe of colour by planting up the bases of two wire baskets and fastening them together (protect the compost in the inverted basket with polythene which can be pulled out when it's in place). Lovely planted up with 'Princess' violas in winter and buzy lizzies in summer.*

And the good news? Winter baskets, except in prolonged dry spells, need no watering at all.

Feeding

The cleverest way of feeding summer baskets is to do it when you're planting up, by adding slow-release fertilizer to the compost. If you use it at the recommended rate, it will keep baskets looking good all season. Alternatively, feed weekly with a high potash fertilizer such as liquid tomato food – but wait for five weeks or so, until the plants have used up all the nutrients in the compost. And more good news – winter displays don't need feeding until the weather warms up in spring.

Deadheading

Removing spent flowers is essential, to keep baskets looking good and to prevent plants from setting seed and giving up the ghost.

An angled hose-lance delivers a fine, penetrating spray with a minimum of effort.

Making the most of Summer Schemes

Summer baskets give you the opportunity to really let rip – to create huge, lush, outrageous plantings in colours as carefully co-ordinated or as madly clashing as you like. And if you enjoy using your garden as a way of expressing yourself, then a hanging basket allows you to make a very bold statement indeed.

Romantic souls are very easy to spot. Their baskets will be dripping with soft, dreamy colours. Rose-pink busy lizzies, pale pink geraniums, white petunias, pastel blue brachycome and a flurry of pale blue lobelia.

Cheery, devil-may-care types just slap the colour in with no regard for any of the so-called 'rules'. Bright orange nasturtiums clash with carmine petunias, red geraniums shriek at electric yellow tuberous begonias – with not a hint of grey or green foliage colour to calm the riot down. But it works. It may not look too coherent from a distance, but it's a wonderfully vibrant, lively picture in close-up.

Fiery temperaments express themselves in hot, bold schemes: blazing reds, flaming oranges, scorching magentas, smouldering purples – a torrid Mediterranean mix. Cooler heads keep it simple; crisp white and blue, with just a few touches of lemon yellow.

Finally there are the minimalists, lovers of order and utter simplicity. Their baskets will be either all one colour (white lobelia and petunias is a classic mix) or a superbly tended planting of

These matching pairs of beautifully planted baskets and urns are dripping with summer flowers and foliage. Set against mellow stone, they make a wonderfully colourful and welcoming display at the entrance to a house.

BACKGROUND RESEARCH

Don't forget to take into account the background against which your basket will be viewed. An all-white basket will disappear on a white-painted wall, while a red basket won't be much of a highlight against red brick. But you can create some terrific effects if you design your basket so that it makes the most of any adjacent colour; if it's next to a bright blue door, make sure to add some blue to the planting mix; if there's a golden climbing rose nearby, include some starry golden bidens in your basket.

Remember, too, that baskets don't necessarily have to be attached to walls. Anything sturdy will do. We've seen some brilliant displays on pergolas, and a basket of shade-loving busy lizzies can look wonderful on a low-slung tree branch.

just one type, and colour, of plant – a neat ball of busy lizzies for instance, or a symmetrical explosion of continental geraniums.

Psychologists reckon they can tell our characters just from little things like the colour and pattern of a man's tie. We reckon they should take a look at our hanging baskets – they'd have a field day.

SUMMER SCHEMES

Above: all strawberries are good news but 'Sweetheart' is especially useful for hanging baskets, with its neat, compact plants, no untidy runners and excellent flavour.

Left: a sunny spot by the kitchen door is the perfect place for high-rise tomatoes. The tangy flavour and aroma of freshly picked tomatoes is unbeatable.

HIGH-RISE SUMMER FEASTS

Have you ever seen a hanging basket planted up with strawberries? The fat dangling fruits look as wickedly tempting as the apple that Adam offered Eve. So much so that in our garden centre days, staff considered it an essential part of their duties to tend the basket strawberries very carefully, and make sure that no fruit was ever allowed to become over-ripe and spoil the display. To grow your own, just plant up three plants in a 25cm/10in basket; a plastic basket is preferable to a wire one because it retains more moisture and strawberries hate to dry out. Placed in a sunny spot and turned regularly for all-round ripening, you'll get excellent crops.

The glowing red globes of basket tomatoes are equally appealing, and the variety to use is 'Tumbler',

specially bred for the purpose. The cherry-sized fruits cascade down the side of the basket, and they're exceptionally tasty. Remember to feed regularly and to keep the compost evenly moist: irregular watering can lead to split (though perfectly edible) fruit.

And how about a herb basket? A mix of young plants can look very attractive, but the most decorative of all is a thyme basket, using forms of the low creeping thyme, *Thymus serpyllum*. Planted in the sides and top of a wire basket, they knit together into a tapestry of leaf colour (green, bronze, gold-variegated), and from June to August the basket is a ball of flower. Great for wildlife gardeners, because butterflies and bees love them. Look out in particular for 'Pink Chintz', 'Russetings', 'Annie Hall' and 'Rainbow Falls'.

Baskets for Shady Spots

The phrase 'hanging basket' instantly conjures up a sunny setting, but there's no reason why you can't create something appealing in a shady spot. You just have to choose your plants rather more carefully.

Defining the degree of shade in which you're gardening is tricky, but let's start with a 'north wall' kind of situation – a spot that gets no sun, or very little, but has an open aspect and isn't directly overlooked by trees or other walls. There are lots of plants you can get away with here.

Ivy, lamium, glechoma (nepeta) and plectranthus are all excellent foliage trailers, with attractive variegations, that will do well. For a flowery infill, busy lizzies and begonias will thrive, and give you access to an enormous colour range. Pansies will be relieved to be away from hot sun and really give of their best – again, your choice of colour is vast, from clear yellows and blues through to pastels and the dusky 'antique' shades. Fuchsias will appreciate the relative cool (they're easily frazzled in sunny baskets), and white/carmine 'Cascade' is one of the neatest and most floriferous. And a haze of lobelia in blue, white or pink will add the finishing touch to a basket that will bring its own sunny good looks to a shady spot.

Deeper shade is the most difficult of all, but you still have access to ivies, lamiums, begonias and busy lizzies. If it sounds a bit dull, just think of the effect you could achieve with, say, a basket planted

Flower pouches create a hanging column of colour, here planted up with a bright mix of shade-tolerant busy lizzies.

up entirely with sizzling red busy lizzies, or a mix of white-variegated lamium and white begonias. Your options may be limited, but a bit of imagination can work wonders.

This bold globe of colour for a shady porch uses deep pink begonias. The fully rounded shape is achieved by wiring two ready planted baskets together.

GERANIUMS

Making the most of Geraniums

Geraniums are terrific plants for all containers, for their reliability and constant succession of flower, but they're especially valuable for baskets because they're one of the most forgiving of all plants if you let them dry out – an important consideration for busy gardeners who need to use plants that virtually look after themselves.

Yes, we should really be calling them pelargoniums, the name they were given 200 years ago, to distinguish them from the true geraniums which are hardy garden plants. But it seems sensible to use the name that's instantly recognizable to most people.

THE BEST FOR BASKETS

Everybody loves the good old **zonal geraniums** – archetypal 'cottage window' plants, with globe-shaped flowerheads and rounded, slightly scalloped leaves which bear (in most instances) a maroon horseshoe-shaped pattern. They're perfect for planting as the centrepiece of a hanging basket, producing a mass of flower from the minute you put them out right through to the first frosts.

Breeders are forever introducing new 'series' (sets of plants of a particular size and growth habit, that vary only in their flower colour), but don't worry too much about which series to go for when choosing a plant at a garden centre. It's highly unlikely that you'll ever find a zonal geranium that won't do you proud, so just pick out the colour that appeals to you and will fit in well with your chosen scheme. The only geraniums that we're not awfully fond of are the doubles; the flowerheads can look just too congested, and they're prone to rotting after rain because they trap the moisture rather than shrugging it off like the singles.

Another group of zonal geraniums are noted for their remarkable leaf colouring (and will also give a good show of flower). The best known is probably 'Mrs H Cox', whose leaves are handsomely patterned green, cream and red/maroon. Or the pretty little 'Happy Thought', with yellow-splashed leaves and bright magenta flowers.

The loose, airy sprays of continental ivy-leaved geraniums create a tumbling cascade of colour.

You'll probably come across **regal geraniums** in your travels too – large, showy flowers, often in attractive colour combinations, and plain green, saw-toothed leaves. 'Lord Bute' is one of the finest, with deep purple flowers edged in carmine. The regals are very desirable in themselves, but you should resist them for baskets. They grow tall and woody, and flower for only a few weeks in late spring and early summer, so they are best suited to patio pots which can be moved out of the limelight after flowering.

For planting up the sides and edges of baskets, the **ivy-leaved geraniums** are perfect, sending out long trails studded, all summer, with posy-like flowerheads. 'Rouletta', with cerise-edged white flowers, is one of the best of the newer varieties, while 'L'Elegante', at well over a century old, is a tried and trusted favourite whose white-edged leaves and palest pink flowers are immensely appealing.

Coming right up to date, the latest ivy-leaved fashion is for the continental types, variously called 'balcon', 'balcony', 'cascade' and 'decora'. These hold their flowers in loose, airy sprays and the effect, especially when several are grown together, is of a tumbling, frothing cascade of colour. Three plants of the same colour in a basket will give you a magnificent display.

WINTER CARE

Most summer bedding plants are annuals, fit only for the compost heap at the end of the season, but geraniums are perennial, and it seems a shame to scrap them when they have the potential for years of reliable flower.

Happy Thought

Mrs H Cox

So, if you've enough windowsill space, bring them indoors for the winter before the first of the frosts. Just dismantle the basket and ease them out with as much root as possible (some damage is inevitable, but rarely fatal). Pot them up so that the rootball makes a pretty snug fit, fill up any gaps with multi-purpose compost, water well and stand them on a light windowsill. You can also cut back any cumbersome growth at this stage.

If they're in a warm room, water them as you would any other houseplant and the zonal types, in particular, will reward you with a winter show of flowers. If they're in a cooler room (an unheated conservatory, for instance), keep them on the dry side and they'll quietly tick over without making much growth until spring.

Increase watering as the weather warms up in spring, and cut back any woody stems by half to encourage new growth from the base. Pinching out the tips of the new growth will also help shape up the plant. By the time it's safe to put them outdoors, you'll have some well-grown plants for instant impact in this year's hanging baskets.

MAKING MORE

Geraniums root quickly and easily from cuttings taken in March, producing sturdy young plants by late May. Take 10cm/4in non-flowering sideshoots, remove the lower leaves and insert them in individual 7.5cm/3in pots. Keep in a warm, light spot and water very moderately. Pinch out the growing tip of new shoots, to keep the plants bushy.

GERANIUMS

Making the most of Easy-Care Baskets

The problem with hanging baskets, as we've said before, is that they do need plenty of tender loving care to keep them flourishing. And, come summer, even the most avid gardener has plenty of other distractions, so it's not entirely surprising that the baskets suffer. But there is a solution — you can have a social life as well as a lovely floral display with an easy-care style of hanging basket.

Nasturtiums and petunias make a cheerful flowering display in a wicker hanging basket and will tolerate brief periods of neglect without suffering a permanent setback.

This is a round-up of all the little tricks you can use to create a basket that won't let you down, even if you neglect it for a short while. And choosing the right plants is your starting point.

Some plants are pretty tough and won't go to pieces if you forget to water them occasionally; they're worth their weight in gold in an easy-care scheme. Others like fuchsias, pansies, lobelia and glechoma (nepeta) are a nightmare if you let them dry out, and will take weeks of pampering to cheer up again. So avoid the prima donnas, pick the plants that will withstand a short period of gardener-induced drought without appearing to suffer at all, and those that will wilt but recover very quickly when watered again.

The all-time best flowering plant for drought-tolerance is, happily, also one of the most desirable of all basket plants – the **geranium** (see p.54). You've probably noticed that a broken shoot will take an age to notice that its water supply has been cut off, and plants in baskets can withstand several days of dryness. **Bidens**, too, is extremely forgiving.

Then there are the flowering plants that wilt when you forget to water them for a couple of days, but will bounce back once watered, without suffering any nasty after-effects. These include **begonia, brachycome, busy lizzie, felicia, nasturtium, petunia** and **verbena**.

Several foliage plants, too, can be relied on to cope well with your sporadic memory loss or long weekends away in high summer. **Helichrysum** and **plectranthus** are the very toughest, but **ivy, lamium** and **lotus** aren't far behind.

BASKETS AND LINERS

Apart from choosing tough plants, there are other ways of making life a little bit easier. When selecting a wire basket, remember that the bigger they are, the better. Larger baskets hold more compost which, despite having more plants in it, dries out less quickly. The largest (40cm/16in) baskets are the best, but they weigh a ton and cost a small fortune to plant up, so we like to strike a happy medium by using the 25cm/14in size baskets.

And yes, even though we much prefer moss-lined wire baskets, they do dry out quickest of all, so in this instance we'd recommend that you use one of the less

TIPS

✔ *Although John Innes composts can make a basket rather heavy, they do hold moisture better than peat-based composts and are easier to re-wet if they've dried out completely.*

✔ *Another ingenious method of conserving water in wire baskets is to place a piece of polythene on the base of the liner and stand a cardboard tube on it. Fill the tube with clay granules, then pack the compost around it. Remove the tube, leaving a central column of granules. Water runs through the granules on to the polythene and is distributed evenly and rapidly throughout the basket.*

attractive but more moisture-retentive wool, foam or fibre liners.

Plastic baskets are far easier to keep moist, especially those which contain a self-watering reservoir which you simply keep topped up. The only problem with these is knowing when the reservoir is running dry. Some models have built-in water indicators but with others you just have to guess – a top-up every two or three days in hot dry weather seems to do the trick. And you can't overwater them, because the manufacturers have cunningly incorporated overflow devices (a grandiose name for little holes at the top of the reservoir).

EASIER WATERING AND FEEDING

You *can* make watering even less of a chore by adding water-retention granules to the compost when planting up. Just mix the sugary granules with water, stir, and they swell into a frogspawn gel which you then add to the compost. There it acts as a reservoir, releasing water as needed.

When it comes to feeding, there are two potential stumbling blocks. Remembering when the next feed is due, and remembering to do it at all. So keep it simple by mixing in slow-release fertilizer granules when planting up. They'll feed the plants all season long, without needing any reminders.

POSITIONING

Finally, the position of the basket makes a difference too. They dry out remarkably quickly in a south-facing spot that gets sun all day; they'll be much less thirsty placed where they'll be in shade for part of the day. And avoid windy positions – wind draws moisture from the leaves and baskets dry out in double quick time.

TOWERING FLOWER-POWER

The beauty of this relatively simple planting is the way in which small-flowered plants have been used to highlight the colours and bold trumpet flowers of the petunias. It will certainly be a most spectacular sight by midsummer.

INGREDIENTS
- 6 x *Petunia* 'Horizon Mixed'
- 10 x *Petunia* 'Chiffon Morn'
- 4 x *Lobelia* 'Lilac Cascade'
- 8 x *Impatiens* 'Accent Mixed' (pink/white selection)

❦ *For real impact, and so that it can be viewed from all angles, hang this flower tower from a sunny pergola.*

❦ *This flower tower has a built-in water reservoir, greatly reducing the frequency of watering.*

Making the most of Winter Baskets

When the first frosts threaten and you dismantle your summer baskets, don't just store them away. Give them a new lease of life by filling them with plants that will provide a succession of colour from autumn right through to spring. They will be wonderfully cheering, even on the most miserable winter's day.

Garden centres are now catering for the ever-increasing demand for winter basket plants, so that when you visit in autumn there's a tempting array of winter-hardy flowers and evergreens at just the right stage for planting out.

WINTER WARMERS

The first winter-warmers to look out for are those that will give real shape and 'presence' to your basket, and you'll find a good choice of small shrubs, such as prettily white- or gold-variegated **euonymus**, and a range of **conifers** from the dumpy to the conical in all shades of green, blue, silver and gold – all of which make splendid centrepiece or 'topknot' plants.

For an attractive trailer that will mimic the full, bushy baskets of summer, you really can't beat that most remarkably versatile plant, **the ivy**. Of the small-leaved varieties that are best suited to baskets, there's a wealth of shapes – arrow-leaved, curled, waved, fingered – and some good variegations. But remember that ivy, like the rest of your winter basket plants, will put on very little growth between October and March, so you'll need several plants for a good, even cover.

Fillers next, and this is where you can start to add some real colour. **Heathers** first, both for their foliage colour (there are some lovely golds and bronzes) and for their spikes of pink and white flower. The new range of 'budding' heathers (producing colourful buds which never actually open) will keep a basket bright from August to December. And for the depths of winter, you can't beat old faithfuls like 'Springwood White', 'Springwood Pink' and 'Pink Spangles'.

BULBS FOR BASKETS

Add a few bulbs to your baskets when planting up – not the tall, large-flowered daffodils or tulips, of course, but the daintier of the spring bulbs. But don't plant them round the sides and base of a wire basket – we tried it once and the effect was decidedly odd as the poor things struggled to grow upwards.

Clumps of double snowdrops are lovely for February flower, together with the richer tones of gold, purple or blue forms of *Iris reticulata*. The small species crocus and blue or white puschkinias will also flower around this time. Follow on in March and April with the larger Dutch hybrid crocus and a sprinkling of deep blue *Scilla siberica*.

And yes, you can have daffodils and tulips, but only the very daintiest: tiny daffodils like 'Lintie', 'Jumblie' and 'Tete-a-Tete', and dwarf tulips such as 20cm/8in 'Chopin', a spring sonata of lemon yellow flushed with red.

A delightful planting for early spring, using delicate trails of silver-variegated Hedera helix *'Glacier' and a bright topknot of 'February Gold' daffodils.*

GOLD-CAPPED WINTER COLOUR

A beautifully colourful winter basket, shading down from the bright gold of variegated euonymus through the rich red berries of gaultheria to the cooler tones of silver-variegated ivy. The gaultheria (partridge berry) is equally useful for its foliage, which takes on warm bronzy tints in winter.

INGREDIENTS
- 1 x *Euonymus* 'Emerald 'n' Gold'
- 5 x *Gaultheria procumbens*
- 5 x *Hedera helix* 'Glacier'

❋ *Gaultheria must have acid conditions to do well, so use an ericaceous compost for this basket.*

❋ *Plant the gaultheria round the sides of the basket and set the ivy in the top, staggering the plants so that they don't directly overhang the gaultheria.*

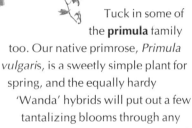

Tuck in some of the **primula** family too. Our native primrose, *Primula vulgaris*, is a sweetly simple plant for spring, and the equally hardy 'Wanda' hybrids will put out a few tantalizing blooms through any mild spells in winter before their main flowering in early spring. Showiest of all, though, are the polyanthus types, with full heads of flower on 15-30cm/6-12in stems; lovely for crowning the top of a basket.

But for really long-lasting colour there's that eighth wonder of the world, the **winter pansy**; how did we ever manage without them? Look for the words 'Ultima' or 'Universal' on the label as a guarantee of winter-hardiness. Plant them up in autumn and they'll bush out and flower while there's still some warmth, carry on through all but the severest winter weather right into spring, when they make a final burst of colour that can last through to May. Virtuous! They come in lovely colours, to suit any scheme. Their charming cousins, the winter violas, have a similarly long flowering period.

And now for something completely different! Use fat, frilly ornamental cabbages and pick up their colour in the dainty infill of winter-flowering heathers, finishing off with a skirt of ivy.

Window Boxes

Window boxes are marvellous – mini-gardens neatly packed in a small space that will brighten up any windowsill or patio. Cram them with summer bedding or fill them with a feast of aromatic herbs or flavour-filled vegetables. Then replant them in autumn to bring some much-needed colour to the drab winter months.

Wooden boxes are especially versatile because you can paint or stain them; choosing a colour that matches the surroundings is a safe option, but you should feel free to experiment with the brighter colours and bold patterns that will keep the less fully planted winter boxes looking good.

The other great thing about window boxes is that, generally, they need a lot less pampering than hanging baskets. So in effect, you get maximum results for minimal effort.

CHOOSING A WINDOW BOX

The first thing to ponder is the size of your window box. The wider and deeper it is, the more compost it can hold and the longer it can be left between waterings. As an extra benefit, plants will establish more extensive root systems and really give of their best.

A minimum depth and width of 20cm/8in is advisable – any smaller than this and plants will dry out pretty quickly in the height of summer and watering could become a real chore.

The length of the box depends on the position you have planned for it, but if it's going to be mounted below the windowsill, it will look neatest if it's just slightly shorter than the sill length. And on a long run of windowsill, it's worth considering whether you'd be better off with two boxes butted together rather than one long box; the single box, filled with compost and plants, will be very heavy if you need to move it.

Window boxes are made in a range of materials, so let's look at the pros and cons of each.

PLASTIC

As we've said before, you get what you pay for when you buy plastic containers – the cheaper they are, the shorter their life expectancy. So go for the best you can afford, and choose one with a thick, solid rim which is less likely to split if handled awkwardly.

Be careful where you place your window box. A large, fully planted box resting on a window-ledge can block a lot of daylight from the room. If the box can be set on brackets so that the top is flush with, or even slightly lower than, the sill, more light can get into the room, and it also overcomes the problem of side-opening windows.

Smaller, less vigorous plants, like these pretty cowslips and violas, are the best choice for thick-walled terracotta window boxes.

The best plastic window boxes will last for years and, if you don't like the look of shiny plastic, can be disguised by popping them into a wooden outer sleeve. These can be bought from most garden centres, or can be made, relatively simply, from marine plywood. This is also a cunning way of hiding the fact that two small plastic boxes have been used instead of one large one.

WOOD

Wooden boxes look lovely, but the range on offer at garden centres is usually rather limited, and they can be

FIXING A WINDOW BOX

It's essential to secure window boxes safely, especially if they're above ground floor level. Most windowsills slope slightly, to shed water. If the slope is steep, cut small wedges of wood to level the box. This also helps air to circulate around the base of the window box, which prolongs the life of wooden boxes and allows water to drain away more easily.

For additional security, use angle brackets to secure the box to the frame or wall. Alternatively, hold them in place by drilling a small hole at either end of the back of the box, attaching eye hooks to the frame or wall and

threading 1mm galvanised wire between the two.

Garden centres sell brackets to hold window boxes in place under sills, with a lip that prevents them from slipping or being knocked off. They're usually purpose-made for plastic boxes but will often fit wooden boxes and some terracotta troughs. Position the brackets so that when you sit the window box on them there is a 10cm/4in overlap at each end, to help distribute the weight evenly. You can also buy special brackets which enable you to hang boxes on railings or from the tops of low walls.

Like a crooked picture, a crooked window box will always offend the eye, so use a spirit level to check that it's absolutely straight before fixing it to brackets secured firmly to the wall below the window.

Using a plastic box as a liner will greatly extend the life of this handsome wooden window box as well as being simpler to plant up.

A painted wooden window box can be a delightful feature in its own right. Note the extra bracket supporting the centre of the box.

very expensive. But if you're a dab hand at DIY, you can get exactly the right size and shape for your windowsill, at an affordable price, by making your own.

Use 23cm/9in planed softwood and cut it to size for the sides, ends and base. Mark, then drill the screwholes, and fix together with brass screws (if your carpentry is up to our standards, a few additional small angle brackets on the inner joins wouldn't come amiss). Drill 13mm/½in drainage holes in the base, allowing two per 30cm/12in of box.

Prime and undercoat the wood before painting with outdoor gloss. For a more natural appearance, use an outdoor wood preservative or stain (making sure that they're not toxic to plants) and waterproof it with a coat of matt polyurethane varnish.

The one problem with wooden boxes is that they slowly deteriorate over the years because the sides and base are in constant contact with moist soil, so check them over very carefully every year to see that they're still strong and firm – a collapsing window box is quite a hazard in a high-rise situation. You can, however, extend their life by doing the actual planting up in an inner plastic trough which gives you the best of both worlds – the look of wood with the longevity of plastic.

TERRACOTTA
Much as we love the look of terracotta window boxes, they should be chosen with care. They are heavy, and the walls are so thick that the smaller ones hold relatively little compost, making watering a nightmare.

FIBRE
Dark brown compressed fibre boxes are cheap, functional and disposable and will only last for a season or two. Their colour and papier maché texture aren't terribly attractive, so they're usually placed, ready planted, into wooden boxes.

CHOOSING A WINDOW BOX

TIPS

✔ *When fixing boxes on brackets below a side-opening window, allow for the height of the plants when calculating the clearance needed for opening the window.*

✔ *Self-watering window boxes are available. They're a wonderful labour saver in summer, but shouldn't be used in winter because plants could get waterlogged.*

✔ *It's best to fix window boxes firmly in position before filling with compost and planting. You may find it extremely difficult doing it the other way around.*

✔ *Don't forget that when you water a window box it will drip. So take care when positioning it or it could be the end of a perfect relationship with the people downstairs.*

GROWING SUCCESS

Growing Success

Well-planted window boxes are a real joy. Plants always look good 'framed' by a window, and you (and anyone passing front-of-house boxes) will get tremendous pleasure from them. Plus, of course, it's the only form of gardening that you can enjoy from your favourite armchair, gazing out at, say, a frieze of tulips in spring, and a row of bright geraniums in summer.

PLANTING UP

First give your plants a good drink, then line the base of the box with a 2.5cm/1in layer of crocks (broken pot) or coarse gravel, to prevent the drainage holes from blocking up with compost.

Half fill with compost, then place your plants in the box and shuffle them round until you get the right mix of heights, colours and textures.

Now fill the box loosely with any good multipurpose compost to within 2.5cm/1in of the rim and remove the plants from their pots (if they're in strips, tease them apart as gently as possible).

TIPS

✔ *Always choose sturdy, healthy plants. If you're confused about how many you might need for a summer display, for instance, or what colours to put together, just take your empty window box along to the garden centre with you. Then you can wander round putting in various plant combinations until you're happy with it.*

✔ *When planting up a box, logic dictates that taller plants should be towards the back, and trailers at the edge, but it's also important that your display is symmetrical. A tall plant at one end looks very odd if there isn't one at the other end, to balance it.*

✔ *If your box is used for a permanent planting, refresh the compost each spring by carefully scraping away and replacing the top layer around the plants.*

✔ *Wall-mounted containers such as hayracks are often used as alternatives to window boxes. For best results, choose the larger models which hold a greater volume of compost.*

Make a hole for each plant and place them in at the same level as they were in the pot, firming the compost around them. Finally, firm down between the plants, adding extra compost to any dips, and water well.

AFTERCARE

Keep boxes well watered through summer; little watering is needed for winter displays. The simplest way of feeding summer boxes is to incorporate slow-release fertilizer when planting up, or you can feed once a week with liquid tomato food after five weeks or so; winter boxes should not be fed until plants are growing away more strongly in spring. Remove spent flowers regularly.

Geraniums, petunias and trailing lobelias are a tried and tested window-box combination that will never let you down.

SUMMER PLANTINGS

Making the most of Summer Plantings

*Like all containers, window boxes really come into
their own in summer, when you can exploit the
wonderfully varied form and colour of bedding
plants, in schemes as simple or as wildly extravagant as you like. And the box doesn't have to be in
a sunny spot to be awash with colour, as our table
of recommended plants for shade (p. 105) shows.*

Any of the bedding plants that thrive in hanging baskets
will be just as happy in window boxes, and you also
have access to a host of larger plants, like
osteospermums, marguerites, fuchsias and nicotianas
that will give extra height and structure to the planting.

*A beautifully balanced planting that radiates out from white and
pale pink to rich crimson and purple.*

ADJUSTING THE HORIZONTAL HOLD

When it comes to putting colours together in window
boxes, you can be as bold or restrained as you like, but
the one thing to remember is that the colour picture
you're painting is inevitably rectangular. So that for real
impact it's important to keep the horizontal colour lines
in balance. To demonstrate what we're talking about,
just imagine a box that's a froth of sweetness and light
from pale pink and white plants at one end and a solid
block of red at the other. It's going to look disturbingly

A DELICIOUS MIX OF PLANTS GALORE

This window box packs a
powerful mixture of plants into
a small space, the colours shading
from central pinks and mauves to
deepest bronze. The ingredients,
moving from left to centre (double
up for a whole box) are:

- 1 x *Heuchera* 'Palace Purple'
- 1 x *Lobelia* 'Blue Cascade'
- 1 x *Begonia*, bronze-leaved selection
- 1 x *Helichrysum petiolare*
- 1 x *Osteospermum* 'Pink Whirls'
- 1 x *Brachycome*, blue form
- 1 x *Pelargonium* 'Caroline Schmidt'
- 1 x *Nemesia* 'Confetti'

LATERAL THINKING

For a fine summer display that won't need replanting each year, turn your window box into a rockery by filling it with alpines. It sounds an odd idea initially, because they're more usually associated with trough and sink plantings – but a window box is, after all, simply a trough in a particular location. The plants will love the baking they'll get on a south-facing window, and the relative protection from winter wet provided by the house.

There's an infinite variety of summer flowering rock plants to choose from, but for reliability and long flowering, we'd especially recommend rock pinks (*Dianthus*), low-growing campanulas, alpine phlox and the bright flowers of rock rose (*Helianthemum*) which are produced in such abundance. And you can take your pick from Best Rockery Plants (see p. 94), almost all of which will love a sunny position.

You won't achieve quite the same impact as you can with bedding plants, but you're going to have a beautiful little garden to enjoy whenever you throw open the window.

Dianthus *'Pike's Pink'*

SUMMER PLANTINGS

---

unharmonious. For a window box that really pleases, you must have balance.

There are several ways of creating this essential symmetry, and the easiest of all is simply to make sure that your chosen mix of plants is evenly distributed throughout the box. A large central geranium, for instance, and one at either end, an evenly mixed infill of smaller plants, plus three trailers at the front to echo the position of the geraniums. It may sound a bit regimented, but once the plants bush out and fill the box, it'll look utterly natural.

Another clever trick is to plant in layers of colour. Have a backdrop of, say, deep purple petunias right across the box, fronted by a line of crimson busy lizzies and deep blue trailing lobelia. Such a hot scheme can be highlighted by a full skirt of lime green trailing helichrysum.

Hardest of all, but one of the most effective if you can manage it, is a colour scheme that radiates out from the centre of the box. Take petunias as a backdrop again, but swop the purple for a deep

Lines of colour run right across this box of ivy-leaved and zonal pelargoniums, from pale salmon-pink through rose-pink to deepest rose.

magenta, and place them in the centre of the box. Surround them with a mix of deep pink flowers (verbenas and a few more petunias, for instance). These can merge with rose pink geraniums towards the sides of the box. And as the finishing touch, plant up the edges with palest pink busy lizzies. Lovely.

SUMMER PLANTINGS

MINI-FARMING

This one's for frustrated vegetable gardeners without a scrap of earth to call their own, or even the tiniest patio or balcony. Provided you've got a sunny windowsill or two, you really can raise excellent crops in window boxes.

Runner beans would be silly of course (you wouldn't be able to see out), and cabbages would occupy far too much space, but there are plenty of small vegetables and salad crops that you can pack into a window box and proudly call yourself a son or daughter of the soil.

Early in the year (March and April), make sowings of those crops that are best suited to relatively cool temperatures, since a sunny window box can be fearsomely hot in high summer. Choose fast-maturing varieties like spring onions, baby carrots, 'Little Gem'

lettuce and mini-beetroots. Speediest of all are radishes: the smaller varieties can be ready in under four weeks, so that you can make a second or even a third sowing. And while all radishes are white-fleshed, they have a wonderful range of skin colours (from the traditional red to white, black and even yellow) that perk up a mixed salad no end.

With the exception of the lettuce, all these crops can be grown 2.5cm/1in apart and should be kept well watered and fed once a week (after the initial six weeks) with a general liquid fertiliser.

By early June, so long as frosts are a distant memory, it's time to harvest your early crops and replant with the fruiting vegetables (raised from seed indoors or bought from the garden centre) that will relish summer heat. Plant breeders now appreciate that gardeners are much more adventurous than they used to be about growing in containers, and each year more and more mini varieties become available. The trailing tomato 'Tumbler' (bred for hanging baskets but great in window boxes too) has been around for a while, and there are now miniature peppers, like 'Redskin', and even tiny aubergines which grow to only 30cm/12in, producing masses of 2.5cm/1in shiny black fruits. And if you've any space left, you can plant up a few dwarf French beans – 'Delinel' is a prolific cropper and supremely tasty.

As with the earlier crops, be sure to keep them well watered, and feed once a week with liquid tomato food. You won't have a freezer full of surplus crops by the end of summer, but you'll have had some very pleasant home-grown tastes to perk up your meals.

Herb farming is another happy pursuit for hungry window box gardeners. Here, staples like sage, chives and fennel are supplemented by decorative nasturtium and sweet cicely (both excellent in salads), plus aromatic plants like lavender and scented-leaf geranium.

MAKING AN IMPRESSION

I f you're expecting important visitors, here's an instant May scheme that will leave them deeply impressed, using the glowing golds of broom and pot chrysanthemums. The colour won't last for more than a month or so, but it's good to be extravagant once in a while.

INGREDIENTS
- 1 x *Cytisus praecox* 'Allgold'
- 2 x *Abutilon,* variegated
- 3 x pot chrysanthemum
- 2 x *Genista lydia*
- 3 x *Hedera helix* 'Eva'

SUCCESS IN SUN OR SHADE

A rich, densly planted box, this one would be just as happy on a north-facing windowsill as on a sunny one. Purple and gold is the theme, and by midsummer the creeping Jenny (*Lysimachia),* trailing between the ivy and lobelia, will be studded with gold buttercup flowers. From left to centre (double the numbers for a complete box), the plants are:

INGREDIENTS
- 4 x pansy, purple and gold selection
- 2 x *Hedera helix* 'Eva'
- 1 x *Helichrysum* 'Limelight'
- 1x *Lysimachia*
- 1 x *Lobelia* 'Blue Cascade'
- 1 x tuberous begonia, pale gold selection

Making the most of Fuchsias

With their heavy flowers carried on slender stalks, fuchsias dance in every breath of wind, and they're shaped pretty much like ballerinas too – with the 'body' formed from the tube and outstretched sepals, the 'skirt' (frilled or plain) from the corolla. And the long, elegant stamens will do as well as anything for legs. Fuchsias are lovely flowers to have about the place.

Fuchsias are perfect plants for window boxes in both sun and partial shade. Grown in pots, the down-turned flowers are hard to appreciate unless you raise them to eye-level, and in hanging baskets they'll turn up their toes if you let them dry out. But in a well-tended window box they can tumble and cascade and show themselves off to their very best advantage.

The showier fuschsias so valued for their summer-long colour are tender (unlike the smaller-flowered

*The spider plant (*Chlorophytum*) contrasts well with the red-ribbed foliage of* Fuchsia *'Thalia' in this magnificent lead box.*

hardy garden varieties) and should never be put out while there's any danger of frost. They do well in sun as long as they're kept well watered but, with very few exceptions, they also thrive in partial shade, so are especially useful for north-facing windows. Apart from never letting them dry out, the other key to success is deadheading. The flowers drop, but they leave behind little seed capsules which are easy to miss until they have turned into the size of a small grape. So rummage around in the foliage and remove them while they're still small.

To keep plants from year to year, pot them up in the same way as geraniums (see p. 55) and place in a cool, frost-free room. Reduce watering gradually, and when the leaves have dropped, reduce it again to an absolute minimum. Wake the plants up in spring when the first tiny leaf-buds appear by slowly increasing the watering, and cut them back to a well-shaped framework. Keep pinching out the growing tips to encourage bushing and pot on in early April, ready for planting out in the first half of June.

Fuchsias have amazing flower power as this window box, still dripping with bloom in October, demonstrates.

BEST FUCHSIAS FOR WINDOW BOXES

Fuchsia *'Marinka'*

Fuchsia *'Thalia'*

Fuchsia *'La Campanella'*

There are any amount of fuchsias that will grow happily in window boxes, so rather than blind you with a flurry of names, we'll pick out just a few that we hope will give you as much pleasure as they give us, and shouldn't be too hard to find.

Annabel
Very large, double blooms of white suffused with pale pink on a bushy plant. Exceedingly romantic.

Cascade
A lovely trailer, very free-flowering, with a pale pink body and single, bell-shaped skirt in deep carmine.

Dancing Flame
Wide, bright flowers, with a pale orange body and orange-carmine petticoat, on a trailing plant.

La Campanella
Small flowers, very freely produced on trailing stems. White body, wide, ruffled rich purple skirt maturing to lavender.

Marinka
A vigorous, cascading plant, the single flowers have a rich red body, magenta skirt and extremely long legs. Rather elegant.

Pink Marshmallow
A popular trailer with large, very fully double flowers shading from a pale pink body to a blush-white skirt.

Thalia
Very long slim tubes of orange-red flowers, produced in clusters on the stem tips, against deep green, red-backed foliage. A very striking upright bush, 'Thalia' is best grown in sun.

Fuchsia *'Pink Marshmallow'*

Making the most of Winter/Spring Boxes

It always seems such a shame that most gardeners don't bother with winter and spring colour in window boxes. The summer display is allowed to peter out, the debris is lifted in autumn and the box left empty until early the next summer. But it takes very little trouble to create a box that will look good from autumn right through to late spring and it really is well worth it. A few minutes' planting will give you months of pleasure.

For an absolute minimum of effort, simply aim at a good spring display by planting up some bulbs. Snowdrops, dwarf reticulata irises and species crocus will make their appearance in February, dwarf narcissi like 'February Gold' and 'Minnow' will give colour in March. For an April splash, some stately hyacinths and perhaps a few tiny tulips like 'Scarlet Baby' – a little gem at only 20cm/8in.

But we bet that after you've planted up, you stare at all that bare earth, with no prospect of greenery until Christmas, and decide to add just a little colour. No harm in that. A couple of small-leaved ivies perhaps, to soften the edges, and maybe a few winter pansies, the odd heather, just one or two polyanthus and forget-me-nots....Before you know it, you'll have planted up a quite substantial box that will need very little care. Just the occasional watering in dry spells, and deadheading as necessary.

And you'll enjoy the resultant display so much that next year you might want to be even more ambitious and add in some evergreen dwarf conifers, or perhaps the boldly cut leaves and saucer-shaped flowers of hellebores. All these will give height and structure to the back of the box and form the perfect backdrop for your pansies, bulbs and a host of other spring flowers.

The next step is to start colour co-ordinating, working out a scheme based on blue and gold, say, or a sparkling green and white. And when you find yourself doing the grand tour of garden centres to get just the right shade of pansy, that's when you realise you've really got hooked on winter window box gardening.

Fabulous russet colours for winter come from skimmia, heather and ornamental kale. For summer colour, simply swop the heathers and kales for dusky 'Antique Shades' pansies.

FROM WINTER INTO SPRING

Bridging the gap between winter and spring, this box features bright-eyed primroses, heathers which have flowered right through winter, and two favourites for year-round interest, conifer and skimmia. For summer colour, swap the heathers and the primulas for easy bedding plants such as busy lizzie and compact varieties of petunia.

INGREDIENTS

- 1 x *Juniperus* x *media* 'Sulphur Spray'
- 2 x *Skimmia japonica* 'Rubella'
- 2 x *Erica carnea* 'Pink Spangles'
- 1 x *Erica carnea* 'Springwood White'
- 2 x hybrid primula

MAKING THE MOST OF YEAR-ROUND COLOUR

It's all very well us advocating that you plant up your window boxes afresh every spring and autumn, to maximise the seasonal displays. But sometimes it's just not a practical proposition; if the box is difficult to reach, for instance, or if you simply don't have the time to spare for looking after these more demanding plants.

The solution is to create a permanent framework of evergreen plants and just pop in a few splashes of seasonal bedding for extra colour, so that once the initial planting is

The ultimate low-maintenance box – a permanent, year-round frill of ivy which plays host to an infill of seasonal plants.

done, there's an absolute minimum of work involved.

To make it even more low maintenance, use evergreens that will take an age to outgrow the box. For the background planting, skimmias are pretty slow-growing, and should last for several years before they're better suited for large pots or for planting out in the garden. Euonymus, too, will inch their way along, and can look very attractive trimmed into little mounds.

Another plant that responds beautifully to clipping is dwarf box (*Buxus sempervirens* 'Suffruticosa'). Balls and lollipops are the standard shapes, but if you set in a few of the younger plants supplied for low edgings, at 15cm/6in intervals along the back and

sides of the box, you would soon have a strikingly formal hedged enclosure for the rest of your displays.

But the slowest of all background plants are the dwarf conifers, in a wealth of shapes and colours. Their growth rate is infinitesimal, and they'll last almost indefinitely in a window box.

For an infill (leaving a few gaps for bedding plants like summer begonias and winter pansies), take your pick from any of the more compact heathers, dwarf hebes, low-growing ajugas and evergreen hardy perennials like *Heuchera* 'Palace Purple' or heavily white-splashed 'Snowstorm'.

And for a permanent cascade at the front of the box, it's our good old dependable friend, the ivy. If you cut back the longest, woodiest stems each spring to promote fresh new growth, the ivies will probably last longer than the window box!

Top Plants

From the vast range of plants that will thrive in the confined situation of pots, tubs, troughs and hanging baskets, this is our personal pick of those that we know will give of their very best.

Best BEDDING PLANTS

❀ BEGONIAS

The fibrous rooted begonias *(Begonia semperflorens)* are wonderful plants and exceptionally neat, growing to only 20cm/8in high. They're invaluable as much for their attractive copper, green or bronze foliage as for their long display of pink, red or white flowers. Good in sun or shade. A very reliable choice for baskets, boxes or tubs. Look out too for the taller tuberous varieties which are discussed in 'Best Bulbs', page 80.

❀ BIDENS

An excellent and extremely colourful trailing plant for hanging baskets. The bright yellow starry blooms appear in abundance all summer against the ferny foliage. It's also remarkably tough and can withstand being dried out for several days – a valuable asset for the absent-minded gardener! If the plant has one fault, it can become just too rampant, so trim it back occasionally.

❀ BRACHYCOME

The Swan River daisy is a charmer for any type of container. Lovely feathery, fresh green foliage and pale purple daisy-like flowers with the rather convenient habit of closing up when watering is overdue. A long-flowering annual for the edges of pots and baskets, to a neat 23cm/9in. Plant breeders are rapidly introducing new colours but, so far, we've seen nothing that beats the original.

Bidens

Brachycome

BEDDING PLANTS

Busy lizzies

Forget-me-nots

❀ BUSY LIZZIE (Impatiens)

Happy in sun or shade and available in over 20 different colours, busy lizzies are one of the very best choices for any container and will flower happily for months. They prefer a moist compost and grow to 15cm/6in or slightly taller, depending on the variety. Their cousins, the sun-loving and taller (45cm/18in) New Guinea hybrids, are best in pots and have glossy, often variegated foliage and large, eye-catching, brilliantly coloured flowers.

❀ DIASCIA

Charming plants, with delicate spikes of flower, and deservedly popular for their remarkably long and vigorous flowering season. All are ideal for containers in sun, growing to around 20cm/8in, and while they may not survive a severe winter, can easily be propagated from cuttings taken in summer. The colour range is rather limited, though, to shades of pink and apricot. A new variety, 'Coral Belle', is reckoned to be one of the very best.

❀ FOLIAGE PLANTS

Use foliage plants to add the finishing touches to baskets and planters. They're a superb foil for flowering plants, and very attractive in their own right. Among the trailing varieties, we especially recommend lotus (cascading filigree silver foliage and, in a good summer, the bonus of red flowers), *Glechoma hederacea* 'Variegata' (usually sold as 'nepeta', with long trails of cream/green variegated leaves), and ivy in all its glorious variety of leaf sizes, shapes and colours. For bushier foliage, look out for plectranthus (lovely cream-variegated leaves and a bit of a trail to it), *Helichrysum petiolare* (striking and vigorous silver-leaved plant, with some very pretty small-leaved, lime-green and variegated forms), and the best of the lamiums, 'White Nancy' (heart-shaped silvery white leaves edged with green and spikes of white flowers in early summer).

❀ FORGET-ME-NOT (Myosotis)

Their popularity seems to have waned in recent years, but we love them. One of the prettiest plants of all for spring pots and tubs, to 30cm/12in. Pink or white varieties are also available, but stick to the blue – it's the perfect companion for taller tulips and daffodils. Look out, too, for the more compact forms which can be teamed up with smaller bulbs. When buying, avoid any plants with yellow or mildewed leaves.

✤ FUCHSIA: see p. 70

✤ GERANIUM
(Pelargonium): see p. 54

✤ LOBELIA

The most popular edging and trailing plant for hanging baskets in sun or partial shade. But they do need looking after – if they dry out, they sulk, and it can take them weeks to recover. The best bush varieties (to 15cm/6in) are 'Crystal Palace' (deep blue with bronzy foliage), sky blue 'Cambridge Blue' and the enchanting sea blue 'Riviera Blue Splash'. The best trailing varieties are the 'Cascade' series, in a wide range of colours.

✤ MARGUERITE
(Argyranthemum)

Few summer plants provide as much colour for as little effort as these beauties. In a sunny spot, most will flower non-stop from June until the first frosts, making

Lobelia

substantial domed plants to 30-60cm/12-24in high. Sadly, they're not hardy, but can be overwintered in exactly the same way as geraniums (see p. 55), and will also root easily from summer cuttings. The best of a lovely bunch are 'Cornish Gold' (very like the old favourite 'Jamaica Primrose', but less inclined to flop about), 'Mary Cheek' (light pink double flowers and grey leaves), 'Peach Cheeks' (peachy apricot, with single and double flowers on the same plant), and 'Royal Haze' (outstanding blue-grey foliage, brilliant white flowers). They're such well-shaped, rounded plants that we like to display them solo, rather than in a mixed planting.

✤ NASTURTIUMS

Among the most attractive and easiest of summer annuals. Just push a few seeds into a hanging basket when you're planting up, or pop them into pots on their own. The climbing forms are a bit too vigorous for mixed plantings, so stick to the more compact (20cm/8in or so) bush types – 'Alaska' has a lovely range of strong colours and white-variegated leaves; 'Empress of India' is a deep velvety crimson with dark foliage; 'Strawberry Ice' is deep yellow, spotted with red.

✤ ORNAMENTAL CABBAGES

You can't beat these for a real splash of colour in autumn and winter. Bred from the edible varieties, there are two main types, both producing large, open heads in a lovely range of white, cream, rose and purple. Kale has deeply cut feathered leaves, and is the hardiest. Cabbages tend to be fuller and more dramatic. A single well-grown plant (23cm/9in high and twice that across) will be a real eye-catcher in a 20cm/8in pot.

Marguerite

Osteospermum

❀ OSTEOSPERMUM

Despite the name, which sounds like a disease, these are lovely plants for a sunny spot, with masses of bright daisy-like flowers with a silky sheen, to 60cm/2ft. One of the best of the old favourites is pale gold 'Buttermilk', while 'Silver Sparkler' is the whitest of whites. Blue-white 'Whirlygig' is a novelty variety with spoon-shaped petals. They're not reliably hardy, so overwinter them like geraniums (see p. 55).

❀ PANSIES (Viola)

Pansies are the absolute stars of winter and spring containers, but in summer they are best used in shady schemes only – they don't cope at all well in hot-spots. Violas have much smaller and more numerous flowers, so are ideal for baskets and boxes that will be seen close up. The pansies, in particular, are available in a tremendous range of colours and patterns, and those with 'faces' are the best choice for pots seen from a distance. The 'Ultima' series (20cm/8in) are the best of the winter pansies and 'Princess' (12.5cm/5in) the pick of

the violas. Both will flower intermittently through winter, depending on the weather, and put on an extra spurt in spring.

For best results, deadhead regularly and feed once a fortnight in spring, using a high potash fertilizer such as liquid tomato food.

❀ PETUNIAS

These have always been superb plants for a sunny spot, but now the plant breeders are making them even better. The popular bush varieties grow to 30cm/12in or so, in a host of colours – go for the singles rather than the doubles, which turn to sodden rags in wet weather. The new 'Fantasy' strain is even neater, growing to half the size of the traditional forms, with masses of flowers all summer. It's the ideal choice for smaller containers. The trailing 'Surfinia' petunias are proven winners for hanging

baskets, with astonishing flower-power and growing to an astounding size (as much as 1.2m/4ft in depth and width), but if space is limited the new 'Million Bells' could be the answer. This is a semi-trailing, compact variety that produces so many tiny bell-shaped flowers that they very nearly hide the leaves.

❀ POLYANTHUS (Primula)

Along with pansies, polyanthus are the showiest of all spring flowering plants. The flowers are held in clusters on tall stems, and are far tougher than the brightly coloured hybrid primroses, which are best grown in a cool room. The hardiest strain of polyanthus is 'Crescendo' (30cm/12in), available in a range of strong colours. Buy them as young plants in autumn and they will quickly establish in containers over winter, bursting into colour in spring.

❀ TOBACCO PLANTS (Nicotiana)

Until recently, tobacco plants have been rather too tall and vigorous for

Pansies (Viola)

Petunias

TIPS

✔ *Most summer bedding plants are tender and although they may be sold early in garden centres, should not be planted out until all danger of frost has passed.*

✔ *Winter bedding plants are the easiest of all to care for, needing only deadheading and the occasional watering in very dry spells. Start feeding once a fortnight in spring for spectacular results.*

✔ *For a semi-shady position, we're great fans of mimulus (the monkey musk) with colourful snapdragon-like blooms. The 'Calypso' series has extra-large 15cm/6in flowers. But be sure to keep the compost moist.*

pots, but the breeders have come up trumps with smaller forms that flower beautifully throughout summer, in sun or part shade, whatever the weather. The 'Domino' series (30cm/12in) is widely available in a range of colours, but the finest new variety is 'Havana Appleblossom' (35cm/14in), white with a rose reverse – simply stunning in containers. But for a real blast of scent, you'll need the taller (60cm/2ft) 'Sensation' varieties.

❀ VERBENA

Very showy summer-flowering plants for sunny positions. The trailing varieties have beautiful ferny foliage and are perfect for baskets or planters. Cerise 'Sissinghurst', soft pink 'Silver Anne' and scarlet 'Lawrence Johnson' (all 23cm/9in) are the traditional favourites. 'Tapien', in pink or violet, is a superb new introduction and 'Pink Parfait' is spectacular, with huge scented flowerheads of light rose pink.

THE BEST OF THE REST

Other summer favourites include the bushy alonsoa (mask flower) which grows up to 60cm/2ft, producing hundreds of spurred flowers all summer, in scarlet, orange and salmon shades. *Solenopsis axillaris* (also sold as laurentia and isotoma) is rapidly becoming a favourite for baskets, with its dome of feathery foliage and bright blue starry flowers (30cm/12in). Among the trailers, look out for *Convolvulus sabatius* with blue trumpet flowers, *Felicia amelloides* 'Variegata', pale blue daisy flowers against green and white foliage, *Scaevola* 'Blue Fan', a vigorous plant with masses of lobelia-like flowers, and *Bacopa/Sutera* 'Snowflake', with flurries of tiny white flowers for months on end. And if you want to see an old favourite in a new light, try a few trailing antirrhinums.

Nicotiana

BULBS

Best BULBS

Allium christophii

Agapanthus

❀ AGAPANTHUS

Imposing summer-flowering bulbs which thrive in pots. The strap-like leaves arch gracefully over the edges of the pot – the perfect foil for the globes of blue bell-shaped flowers from July to September. The robust 'Headbourne Hybrids' (90cm/3ft) are available in a range of blue shades, while the bright blue 'Lilliput' is rather neater at 45cm/18in. For maximum effect, plant in clumps; three bulbs are ideal for a 30cm/12in pot.

❀ ALLIUM

These ornamental onions flower in May and June, providing lovely mid-season colour. The taller varieties are wonderfully architectural; *Allium christophii*

grows to 45cm/18in, topped by a huge ball of star-shaped silvery lilac stars. Among the shorter varieties, *Allium karataviense* is stunning, with broad grey-green hosta-like leaves which contrast beautifully with the ball of dusky pink flowers. Lovely grown with silver/grey foliage plants or white flowers.

❀ BEGONIA

Tuberous begonias produce a magnificent display of colour all summer long, in sun or shade, but they must be kept moist and, as they're tender, should be planted out when all danger of frost has passed. 'Non-stop' varieties are the best for pots, producing masses of really big (7.5cm/3in)

BULBS

Narcissi

Crocus etruscus *'Zwanenburg'*

double flowers on 25cm/10in plants, with a range of vibrant colours. The trailing/pendulous types look superb in hanging baskets. Save the tubers at the end of the season to grow on the following year.

✿ CROCUS

These are real gems, easy to grow and one of the most cheering sights of early spring. They're great value for money, too. For really early flowers, plant either *Crocus chrysanthus* varieties like the pale yellow 'Cream Beauty', or species crocus (light violet *Crocus etruscus* 'Zwanenburg' is mouthwatering). At 5-12cm/2-5in, they're ideal for window boxes and smaller pots. In larger pots, plant in clumps for maximum impact.

✿ DAFFODILS (Narcissi)

One of the most popular bulbs for containers, and no wonder – they're tough, reliable and unbeatable for their colourful display which peaks in March. Dwarf varieties are perfect for pots, baskets and window boxes, and there are some

real beauties to choose from: early flowering 'February Gold' (30cm/12in), multi-headed golden yellow 'Tete-a-Tete' or even sturdier 'Jumblie' (23cm/9in). The creamy-white, lemon cupped 'Minnow' (15cm/6in) is particularly lovely. In larger pots, in a sheltered position where the taller stems won't be buffeted by wind, April-flowering 'Geranium' (35cm/14in), with multiple heads of white, orange/red cupped scented flowers, is a beauty. And the scented May-flowering 'Actaea' (40cm/16in), with its fluttering white petals and tiny red-rimmed 'eye', is our all-time favourite.

✿ HYACINTHS

Hyacinths provide a breathtaking display of colour in April, and an equally breathtaking scent. To

make the most of the solid mass of colour, plant several to a pot, of a single colour – different colours flower at different times. Growing to 25cm/10in, the heavy flowerheads can snap in strong winds, so choose a sheltered spot. Go for the biggest bulbs (17.5cm/7in in circumference) which produce the biggest flowers. Handle the bulbs with gloves if you have sensitive skin.

✿ IRIS

Spring iris are the most delightful of small bulbs, flowering as early as February. The sweetly scented yellow *Iris danfordiae* grows to only 10cm/4in, while the slightly taller *Iris reticulata* varieties (15cm/6in) cover virtually every shade of blue – sky blue 'Harmony' and the darker blue 'Edward' are among the most

BULBS

desirable. Ideal companions for other plants, they look best planted in clumps rather than dotted around.

❀ LILIES (Lilium)

Lilies are the stars of the summer-flowering bulbs – flamboyant, colourful, and remarkably easy to grow. They're perfect for pots that are at least 30cm/12in deep, and three bulbs will provide a magnificent display in a 25cm/10in pot, using a well-drained compost. The easiest to grow are the Asiatic Hybrids such as orange 'Enchantment' and white 'Mont Blanc' (both 75cm/2ft 6in). A dwarf strain has recently been introduced, bred specially for containers, with large flowers but more compact (30cm/12in) stems – two to look out for are 'Red Carpet' and 'Orange Pixie'. But one of the most glamorous of all is the beautifully scented deep pink Oriental Hybrid 'Star Gazer'. It's a 90cm/3ft stunner, and one of the few lilies that prefer a lime-free (ericaceous) compost. Taller varieties may need staking, to hold up the heavy heads of flower. Feed lilies fortnightly with liquid tomato food after flowering, and renew (top-dress) the top layer of compost each spring, to ensure an even better display the next year.

❀ SNOWDROPS (Galanthus)

One of the earliest of spring flowers, ideal for containers in sun or shade, they'll brighten up the dullest

Iris reticulata

of spots. Pop them in small clumps among other plants or in little terracotta pots on their own. The single snowdrop, *Galanthus nivalis,* is slightly more refined than the double-flowered *Galanthus nivalis* 'Flore Pleno'; both are 12cm/5in high. When buying bulbs, check the packet to ensure they have come from cultivated stocks rather than collected from the wild.

Lilies planted with busy lizzies

Snowdrops

TIPS

✔ *In colder areas, to protect against frost damage, use well insulated pots such as wood, terracotta or stone, at least 30cm/12in deep, and plant the bulbs slightly deeper than normal.*

✔ *Most spring bulbs, and daffodils in particular, can be left in the container for years. Summer bedding can be planted over the larger, more deeply planted bulbs. Tulips and hyacinths, however, rarely flower well for a second year in a pot, so are best transferred to the garden.*

✔ *The dying foliage of bulbs can look pretty scruffy, but leave it on for at least six weeks after flowering to build up the bulb's strength for next year's flowers.*

✔ *For a long-lasting spring display, put two or more types of bulb in the same container. Plant a central group of tulips or daffodils, for instance, with an outer circle of crocus or other small bulbs. Tulips and low-growing, starry* Anemone blanda *look particularly good together.*

Spring containers filled with tulips

❀ TULIPS

For a magnificent long-lasting display, these are possibly the finest and certainly the showiest of all spring bulbs. There's a tulip to suit everyone, in a glorious range of colours and styles, from the quietly simple to outrageous show-offs like the 'parrot' tulips. Heights vary tremendously, and the really tall varieties, growing to over 60cm/2ft, are generally better planted in the garden rather than in pots. Pick your bulbs to provide a succession of colour. Among the best of the smaller types are the March-flowering Kaufmanniana varieties such as lemon-yellow 'Chopin' (20cm/8in), which has attractively striped foliage, as have the magnificent April/May-flowering Greigii range which includes the stunning 'Red Riding Hood' (15cm/6in). For larger pots, try double pink 'Peach Blossom' (25cm/10in), pure white 'Athleet' (45cm/18in), rose-red multi-headed 'Toronto' (30cm/12in) or, for later flower, the sugary pink, peony-flowered 'Angélique' (40cm/16in). But really, you can't go wrong with tulips, whatever variety you choose, so select the height and the colours you prefer, plant them up in autumn then sit back and enjoy the spring show.

Best CLIMBERS

CLIMBERS

Clematis *Arctic Queen*

❀ CLEMATIS

Large-flowered hybrid clematis are the best for containers and the most compact are the early types, flowering May/June with a second flush in late summer. Especially good are 'Daniel Deronda' (semi-double blue-purple), 'Sunset' (reddish pink) and 'Arctic Queen' (double white). All grow, with support, to 1.5m/5ft in two years and are suitable for any aspect. Avoid rampant species like *Clematis montana*, which soon become potbound. Grow in pots at least 30cm/12in across and 45cm/18in deep, and plant 10cm/4in deeper

than they were in the original pot, to encourage extra growth buds.

❀ HEDERA (Ivy)

Tough, evergreen self-clinging climbers (also grown as trailers) for sun or shade. Plant in pots at least 25cm/10in wide. The slowest growing are the small leaved forms like silver and white 'Glacier', gold-variegated 'Goldheart', and 'Buttercup', a beautiful butter gold that colours best in sun. For large leaves but a restrained habit, gold-variegated 'Sulphur Heart' is outstanding. Ultimate heights from 1.8m/6ft to 4.8m/16ft.

❀ LONICERA (Honeysuckle)

Beautifully scented, and tough, growing to around 3m/10ft in tubs at least 40cm/16in in diameter. For sunny spots, plant the very free-flowering maroon and cream 'Serotina' or white and yellow 'Halliana'. *Lonicera x americana* is excellent in sun or part shade, with pink/cream flowers from June to November. In smaller containers, try 'Honeybush' at just 1.2m/4ft. All honeysuckle twine, and will need supporting.

❀ PARTHENOCISSUS (Virginia creeper)

Superb self-clinging climbers for sun or shade, with spectacular autumn colour. Best in containers at

least 45cm/18in wide. The most striking is *Parthenocissus henryana*, with dark green leaves veined in silver; much more restrained than *Parthenocissus quinquefolia* which can reach 4.8m/16ft or more in a pot. The finest autumn colour is produced by the similarly rampant *Parthenocissus tricuspidata* 'Veitchii'.

❀ PASSIFLORA (Passion flower)

Beautiful and vigorous climber for a sunny, sheltered spot. The most popular and hardiest variety, *Passiflora caerulea*, produces its remarkable blue and white flowers from June to September. 'Constance Elliott' is another excellent form, with superb ivory white flowers. Ideal for containers at least 30cm/12in wide and grows (with support) to 4.5m/15ft. Protect from severe frost with fleece.

Passiflora

CLIMBERS

✔ Some climbers need support, in the form of canes, wires, trellis or netting. If you don't want to bother with these, choose a self-clinging climber like ivy or parthenocissus (Virginia creeper), which will cling to walls or fences unaided.

✔ Clematis love a cool, moist root-run, so place the pot where it's shaded from sun, and keep well watered through any dry spells. If clematis wilt strikes (the plant collapses very quickly), cut back all top growth and keep your fingers crossed for new growth from the base – the odds are better than the National Lottery.

✔ When training climbers on a trellis, tie them in with soft string or loosely knotted wire ties. Firmer ties can bite into the stems as they grow. Inspect the ties regularly and adjust or renew them as necessary, especially if the plant is situated in an exposed, windy position.

❀ PYRACANTHA (Firethorn)

An easy to grow evergreen wall shrub for sun or shade, with white flowers in early summer followed by colourful autumn berries. Good in containers at least 40cm/16in wide. 'Mohave' is one of the finest: disease-resistant, with heavy crops of orange-red berries, to 1.8m/6ft.

If you fancy red berries, grow 'Watereri'; for yellow berries, 'Soleil d'Or'. Trim after flowering if you want to keep them neat, and beware the fearsome thorns.

ROSES

Climbing roses are included in Best Roses, page 96.

Pyracantha

SWEET PEAS AND OTHER ANNUALS

Few plants could be as easy, as fast or as pretty as the climbing sweet peas. Grow them up a wigwam of canes in a half-barrel from seed sown directly into the compost in March. Keep well watered and do keep picking the flowers for the house – it'll prompt them to produce more. Another fast-growing annual is the climbing nasturtium – plenty of vivid colour, and the peppery leaves and flowers are good in salads. And *Cobaea scandens*, the cup and saucer vine, with purple 'cups' on greeny-white 'saucers' from May to October. All these annuals need a sunny position.

❀ WISTERIA

This classic climber for a sunny position can be grown in a 40cm/18in pot or half barrel, in which the least rampant form,

Wisteria floribunda will reach around 3.6m/12ft. Buy a grafted plant to ensure flowering from a young age, and provide wall-trained plants with very firmly fixed supports, to cope with the weight of the thick, woody stems. For prolific flower, prune twice a year, cutting the long whippy sideshoots back to within 15cm/6in of the main stems at the end of July, and pruning back again to two buds from the main stem in February. For truly enormous flowers, look out for 'Multijuga' (also sold as 'Macrobotrys'). The lilac-blue trails can be over 75cm/2ft 6in long – a spectacular sight in early summer.

Sweet peas

CONIFERS

Best CONIFERS

We've given approximate heights after ten years. And we're sorry about all the long names, but we don't want you to get your *Chamaecyparis lawsoniana* 'Nana' mixed up with *Chamaecyparis obtusa* 'Nana' or even *Chamaecyparis pisifera* 'Nana'.

❀ CHAMAECYPARIS (Cypress)

Some of the very best conifers for containers, in sun or part shade, with a wealth of handsome dwarf varieties to choose from. The best of the smallest include *Chamaecyparis lawsoniana* 'Aurea Densa', a beautiful golden yellow rounded bush to 45cm/18in, while its close relation 'Minima Aurea' is just as lovely but with a pyramidal shape. *Chamaecyparis obtusa* 'Nana Gracilis' is more conical, with deep green foliage neatly arranged in scalloped sprays, to 60cm/2ft. For bigger pots, *Chamaecyparis lawsoniana* 'Ellwood's Pillar' makes a fine column of feathery blue foliage to 90cm/3ft, and the closely related 'Ellwoodii' is a magnificent grey-green pyramid to 2.1m/7ft, turning steely blue in winter: the perfect centrepiece for a large tub.

❀ JUNIPERUS (Juniper)

Tough and hardy, tolerant of partial shade, but particularly good for very sunny positions. They also cope better than most other conifers with drought – this alone should endear them to any container gardener. One of the finest is a real dwarf, *Juniperus communis*

Pinus mugo *'Humpy'*

'Compressa', which forms an extremely narrow column of dense grey-green foliage 45cm/18in high. For a compact, bushy variety, *Juniperus squamata* 'Blue Star' takes some beating – deep blue in winter changing to brilliant silvery blue in summer, at 45cm/18in. For bright golden yellow foliage all year, a compact new introduction, *Juniperus* x *media* 'Gold Sovereign' (60cm/2ft) is a good choice, and looks especially handsome in a container on its own.

❀ PINUS (Pine)

Dwarf pines make excellent container plants but, as they are usually grafted plants, are more expensive than most other conifers. The most compact form of the mountain pine is *Pinus mugo* 'Humpy', a dense, mounded green bush to 30cm/12in. Our favourite, *Pinus mugo* 'Winter Gold', is dark green with gold-tipped needles and turns golden yellow in winter (60cm/2ft). All pines grow best in full sun.

❀ TAXUS (Yew)

Unusually for conifers, yew actually thrives in shade, though it's quite happy in sun too. Most of

Chamaecyparis obtusa *'Templehof*

TIPS

✔ *For maximum winter interest, group contrasting container-grown conifers together – a deep green spire, for instance, looks terrific with a golden pyramid and a bright green globe.*

✔ *When looking around the garden centre for suitable container conifers, search out any with one of the following words in the name – 'Nana', 'Minima', 'Pumila', 'Compacta', 'Compressa' and 'Pygmaea'. They all basically mean that's it's going to be a very small plant indeed.*

✔ *Most conifers will grow happily in any good, well-drained compost, but two families, the spruces* (Picea) *and pines* (Pinus) *need a lime-free ericaceous compost in order to give of their best.*

them are also very slow growing, so they are especially good choices for containers. A form of the Irish yew, *Taxus baccata* 'Standishii', is a particular classic, forming a narrow column of beautiful gold foliage to 1.5m/5ft. The dramatically dark green form, *Taxus baccata* 'Fastigiata', is slightly faster and taller at 1.8m/6ft. The common yew, *Taxus baccata*, so often used for hedging, will grow even larger, but is great if you want to have a go at potted topiary and shape it into balls and pyramids. One word of caution with yews: the berries are poisonous.

❦ THUJA (Thuya)

Similar to chamaecyparis in many ways, except that they do prefer full sun, there are some wonderful shapes, sizes and colours to choose from. *Thuja orientalis* 'Aurea Nana'

Densely conical Juniperus chinensis *'Obelisk' dominates this attractive winter grouping of dwarf pine, prostrate tsuga and creeping juniper.*

(60cm/2ft) is stunning, forming a round-topped oval bush that is rich golden yellow in early summer, turning yellow or bronze-green in winter. For larger containers, *Thuja occidentalis* 'Rheingold' is a popular choice, a rounded cone with bright golden yellow foliage in summer, turning rich coppery bronze in winter, growing to 90cm/3ft. Or opt for *Thuja occidentalis* 'Holmstrup', a narrow cone of rich green foliage to 1.8m/6ft.

THE BEST OF THE REST

Dwarf Japanese cedar *Cryptomeria japonica* 'Vilmoriniana' (30cm/12in) grows into a neat globe of dense foliage, bright green in summer, turning deep rust red in winter. Of the spruces, *Picea glauca albertiana* 'Conica' makes a dense pyramid of bright grass green, slowly reaching 60cm/2ft, while its smaller counterpart, 'Laurin' grows to 30cm/12in and is ideal in a sink or trough garden. All are best in sun.

FRUIT

Best FRUIT

❀ APPLES

Bush apple trees grafted onto semi-vigorous MM106 rootstock are ideal for larger pots and tubs in sun. Regular pruning is essential for good crops, and helps restrict the height to 1.2m/4ft or so. Even more space-saving are the columnar forms, including the 'Minarettes' which are vertical cordons of popular varieties and need only minimal pruning, while 'Ballerinas' need no pruning at all. Both types reach around 1.8m/6ft in pots. Most apples need another compatible apple or crab apple nearby, for cross-pollination. 'Arthur Turner' is one of the best cookers, and 'Falstaff', 'Fiesta', 'Greensleeves', 'Lord Lambourne', 'Sunset' and 'Worcester Pearmain' are all excellent eaters.

Apples grown in a generous wooden container

❀ CHERRIES

Like apples, cherries can either be grown as a 1.2m/4ft bush (on a 'Colt' rootstock) or as a Minarette column to 1.8m/6ft. And both forms are conveniently small enough to fling some netting over when the ripe fruit is under attack from birds. Try 'Morello', the dark red cooking cherry that's good for a north or east wall, or the juicy eaters 'Stella' and 'Sunburst' in a sunny spot. All of these are self-fertile.

❀ ORANGES AND LEMONS

Set outdoors in a sunny spot in summer and given frost protection in winter (min 10°C/50°F), these are

FRUIT

Lemons

Strawberries

highly decorative plants, with some varieties rarely out of flower or fruit. Grow in lime-free ericaceous compost and feed once a week all year round – Chempak No3 in autumn and winter, Chempak No2 in spring and summer. The calamondin orange is naturally dwarf and bushy, while for bigger containers 'Meyer's Lemon' is particularly good.

❀ PEACHES

Peaches need a warm, sheltered, sunny position to do well. And they'll do even better if you can overwinter them in an unheated greenhouse or conservatory where the flowers, which appear early, will be protected from frost. When the flowers do appear, hand-pollinate them with a small paintbrush, because the usual pollinating insects aren't around early in the year. Good varieties are 'Peregrine', 'Rochester' and the smaller (75–90cm/2ft 6in–3ft) 'Garden Lady'.

❀ PEARS

Grown as a bush on 'Quince C' dwarfing rootstock, pears in tubs will eventually reach 1.5m/5ft or more, though they're also available as 1.8m/6ft Minarettes (see 'Apples'). They need a sheltered, sunny position and aren't happy in colder areas, so always check whether they can be grown successfully in your locality. You'll need two varieties to cross-pollinate, and even 'Concorde', said to be self-fertile, will crop better with another variety close by. Other top choices: 'Beth' and 'Conference'.

❀ PLUMS

Plums are easy to grow and almost all are self-fertile, but they do flower early so need a sheltered position to do well. Bush forms grown on 'Pixy' rootstock will reach 1.5m/5ft tall and wide but, again, Minarettes (1.8m/6ft) are available. Two of the best self-fertile eating varieties are purple 'Victoria' and golden 'Ouillins Gage'.

❀ STRAWBERRIES

Strawberries are the most popular of all container-grown fruits – because they're cheap to buy, easy to grow, look pretty, and you can get wonderful crops in pots, window boxes, hanging baskets or growbags (10 plants will fit very happily in one bag). Give them a sunny spot, and keep well watered and fed once a fortnight with a high potash fertilizer such as liquid tomato food from the start of growth in spring until the end of August. Remove any runners as they appear, and replace the plants and compost after two years (they run out of steam). Among the best summer-fruiting varieties are 'Bounty', 'Tenira' and 'Symphony', while 'Aromel' and 'Mara des Bois' will crop twice a year.

Victoria plums

HARDY PERENNIALS

Best HARDY PERENNIALS

Ajuga reptans *'Multicolor'*

❀ AJUGA (Bugle)

Wonderful edging plants, forming low mats of year-round colour in containers and baskets. With pretty, variegated leaves and short (15cm/6in) spikes of blue flower in spring, they're happiest in moist soil in sun or shade. 'Rainbow' is an atttractive mix of cream and pink, 'Braunherz' a fine purple-bronze, and the large-leaved, dark green 'Jungle Beauty' is especially striking for winter baskets.

❀ ALCHEMILLA (Lady's mantle)

One of our all-time favourites, with mounds of fresh green scalloped leaves and loose sprays of tiny yellow/green flowers in mid-summer. *Alchemilla mollis* is the best known, growing to 45cm/18in in sun or shade; cut it back after flowering for a fresh crop of leaves. Smaller forms such as *Alchemilla alpina* are less commonly available but just as desirable.

❀ ARTEMISIA (Wormwood)

Fabulous silver filigree foliage that provides a perfect foil for other plants in a hot, sunny position. 'Powis Castle' is one of the best, but large (1.2m/4ft), so the dwarf, mound-forming *Artemisia schmidtiana* 'Nana' may be more suitable at only 15cm/6in. Both varieties can get rather straggly, so trim the plants back by about half each spring, in order to keep them in shape.

❀ ASTILBE

Ideal for partially shaded positions, with fern-like foliage and feathery plumes of red, pink or white flowers in high summer. Very reliable as long as they don't dry out. 'Bressingham Beauty' is a medium-sized classic with pure pink flowers to 90cm/3ft; tiny 'Sprite', growing to only 25cm/10in, has a profusion of pearl pink flowers and bronze-green foliage.

Geranium cinereum *'Ballerina'*

❀ GERANIUM (Cranesbill)

These are the true geraniums – their tender bedding cousins are actually pelargoniums. Tough and hardy, virtually all of them are gems. 'Wargrave Pink' bears salmon pink flowers all summer, to 40cm/16in, 'Buxton's Variety' has white-centred blue flowers to 30cm/12in, and both are good in sun or partial shade. 'Ballerina' is more of a sun-lover, with lilac-pink flowers finely veined with purple, to 10cm/4in.

❀ HEATHERS

Invaluable small plants for winter and spring displays, these tough evergreen perennials can flourish for years, so long as you trim them

TIPS

✔ *One large and very colourful form of heather,* Erica gracilis, *is sold only in autumn. The reddish purple flowers look magnificent, the perfect centrepiece for a basket or pot, but sadly the plant isn't hardy and rarely lasts beyond December.*

✔ *When choosing* Helleborus orientalis, *try to buy it in flower - most are grown from seed, and both flower colour and the patternings can vary considerably from plant to plant.*

✔ *For a really eye-catching display, plant the vigorous* Houttuynia *'Chameleon' in a pot on its own. The leaves are an amazing aromatic patchwork of yellow, green, bronze and red. Happy in sun or partial shade, it must be kept moist. 20cm/8in.*

Helleborus orientalis

Heuchera '*Palace Purple*'

back after flowering. Our favourites, the *Erica carnea* varieties, combine winter flowering with attractive foliage – 'Vivellii', for instance, with bronze green foliage and carmine flowers, 'Ann Sparkes' with orange-red foliage and purple-red flowers, both to 25cm/10in. Although *Calluna* heathers flower in summer, the best varieties also provide winter foliage interest – 'Robert Chapman' is outstanding, turning fiery orange-bronze in winter. Look out for the 'budding' callunas, too, like the deep red 'Alexandra' which stays in colourful bud from August to December. All heathers are best in sun.

❀ HELLEBORES

These are the plants to cheer you through late winter and spring. The white Christmas rose *(Helleborus niger)* is tricky to grow, so try the lovely Lenten roses *(Helleborus orientalis)*, with colours ranging from white to deep plum purple (30cm/12in). For spring interest, *Helleborus foetidus* (60cm/24in) bears huge heads of yellow-green

flower. All are best in shade and moist soil.

❀ HEUCHERA

Excellent foliage plants, forming neat, virtually evergreen mounds. 'Palace Purple' is a deep purple-bronze with slender spikes of creamy flowers to 45cm/18in. 'Pewter Moon' has pewtery silver leaves with a red reverse, and the pink flowers are a bonus (25cm/10in). Grow in sun or partial shade.

❀ SALVIA

Long flowering, sun-loving and drought resistant, these are classic plants for containers. 'Lubecca' is a compact bushy plant with 45cm/18in spikes of rich violet flower from June to August, which contrast well with yellow flowers. 'Cambridge Blue' needs over-

wintering indoors but it's a treasure, with breathtaking flowers of soft azure blue to 60cm/2ft.

Note: Other favourite hardy perennials, including hostas, ferns, bamboos and grasses, are discussed on pages 28-9, 34-5.

Houttuynia '*Chameleon*'

HERBS

Best HERBS

Basil

❀ BAY

A handsome evergreen tree that can reach dizzy heights in the garden, but is very biddable in pots in a sunny, sheltered position. It's slightly tender, so cover it with horticultural fleece if severe frosts are forecast. Trained plants (usually pyramids or lollipops) should be clipped twice a year, in mid-spring and late summer.

❀ BASIL

An essential ingredient for many Italian dishes, this highly aromatic herb does especially well in pots (12.5cm/5in is ideal) in a warm, sheltered spot. It's a tender annual, so don't put it outside until well into June when the nights are warm. In colder areas, it will do better on a sunny windowsill indoors. Pinch out regularly to encourage bushy growth and keep it on the dry side.

❀ CHIVES

Easy to grow, in sun or partial shade, but they do like to be kept well watered. Cut the reed-like leaves when still young, for optimum flavour. Let them flower, too – the mauve pompons are very pretty. Divide the clumps every three years or so; the bulbous bases are easy to separate.

❀ FENNEL

One of the tallest herbs (to 1.2m/4ft), a beautiful feathery-leaved hardy perennial that looks splendid in 30cm/12in pots in a sunny spot. In addition to the green variety, there are some very pretty bronze-leaved forms that are just as tasty (it's rather like dill, wonderful on grilled fish). The seeds, too, have a refreshing aniseed flavour.

❀ MARJORAM/OREGANO

Sweet marjoram *(Origanum majorana)* is the most commonly grown but is best treated as an annual, while common marjoram *(Origanum vulgare)* is a much hardier perennial. This is best grown in 20cm/8in pots in a sunny spot, although the lovely yellow-leaved forms prefer a little shade from midday sun. Trim over after flowering to promote new growth.

Rich pickings from a wooden trough crammed with a selection of herbs.

❀ MINT

One of the toughest of perennial herbs, mint is very invasive so is best grown in pots on its own, in sun or part shade. Keep the compost moist at all times – place saucers under the pot in summer and keep them topped up with water. Apple mint has soft grey-green leaves and wonderful flavour, and the white-variegated form is even prettier. Spearmint's good, too.

❀ PARSLEY

Parsley is best treated as an annual (in sun or partial shade) stocking up afresh each year. Buy it potted, or for good germination from seed, put it in a sieve and trickle water through all night before sowing. For a garnish, use the curly-leaved form, but for flavour you can't beat flat-leaved French parsley.

❀ ROSEMARY

A fine evergreen but slightly tender, so may need winter protection in colder areas. Plant in spring, in 30cm/12in containers, so that it can get established in a sunny, sheltered spot over summer. Pick regularly to keep neat, but it does eventually become woody and leggy and will need replacing every few years. The tall, elegant 'Miss Jessopp's Upright' grows to 1.2m/4ft.

❀ SAGE

The plain grey-green sage is the best known, but there are some very attractive gold-variegated and purple-tinged alternatives. An evergreen perennial, sage looks equally good in a mixed planting or in a 20cm/8in pot on its own. Grow in sun, and trim lightly in July after flowering. It eventually becomes woody, but is easily replaced from cuttings rooted in water.

❀ THYME

Thymes are valuable evergreens, forming small neat mounds. The common thyme, *Thymus vulgaris*, has the best all-round flavour, although lemon thyme, *Thymus citriodorus*, is wonderful with chicken or fish. Grow in 20cm/8in pots in sun, and trim over after flowering to encourage dense, bushy growth. Like rosemary and sage, thyme does not age gracefully, and should be replaced every few years.

Thymes in a herb pot

Parsley

TIPS

✔ We don't advise growing parsley in special 'parsley pots' with side planting holes. It never does well in them because they dry out too quickly, are difficult to water and don't allow a big enough root system to develop.

✔ To grow a standard bay tree from scratch, start with a young tree with one straight main stem. As it grows, cut off the lower sideshoots, leaving the top to develop. When the tree is 20cm/8in taller than you want, pinch out the top leading shoot and allow the ball of foliage to grow.

✔ Aromatic, mat-forming camomile is a lovely evergreen herb for containers. 'Flore Pleno' has double white flowers and the prettier-leaved non-flowering 'Treneague' looks rather good with spring bulbs.

ROCKERY PLANTS

Best ROCKERY PLANTS

❀ CAMPANULA (Bellflower)

Summer-flowering gems that are very easy to please in a sunny position. Blue or white flowered *Campanula carpatica* is relatively vigorous, forming spreading mounds of neat foliage to 15cm/6in, covered in beautiful cup-shaped flowers from June to August. The very similar blue-flowered 'Dickson's Gold' has golden-yellow foliage which is best shaded from midday sun.

❀ CORYDALIS FLEXUOSA

This is a plant that everyone falls in love with. The form 'China Blue' is the best, with sheets of scintillating blue flowers through April and May. Remarkably, it's in leaf from November to June, and lovely fresh green, delicate foliage it is too. Grow in sun or shade in 20cm/8in pots and keep the compost moist. 30cm/12in.

❀ DIANTHUS (Pinks)

Real charmers – most are scented, with silvery or bluish evergreen foliage in tufted mats. Best in full sun and well-drained soil. 'Inshriach Dazzler' forms neat mounds of vivid carmine pink and 'Pike's Pink' is a tidy little plant with large pink semi-double flowers (both to 10cm/4in). *Dianthus deltoides* 'Albus' has white flowers and fine grasslike foliage and is slightly taller at 15cm/6in.

❀ HELIANTHEMUM (Rock rose)

Quick growing and extremely colourful bushy evergreens. Flowering first in early summer, they can be clipped back by half to flower again. A sunny spot is essential, as is a well-drained compost. 'Wisley Pink' has soft pink flowers which contrast beautifully with the grey foliage. 'Wisley

TIPS

✔ *The best time to buy alpines is generally in spring, when garden centres have their widest selection on sale. And since most alpines grow very quickly, save money by buying the smaller, rather than the more mature, plants.*

✔ *Clump-forming rockery plants can deteriorate if not dug up and divided into smaller pieces every few years. Do this in spring – it rejuvenates the plants and you get a few extra to give away to friends.*

✔ *The one thing most rockery plants hate is to get too wet in winter, so check that the pots are draining properly each autumn and keep them free of fallen leaves. Placing terracotta feet under pots is an extra precaution against waterlogging.*

Helianthemum *'Wisley Primrose'*

Phlox subulata *'White Delight'*

Primrose' has larger, soft yellow flowers. Both grow to around 20cm/8in.

❋ LEWISIA

Among the most spectacular of alpines, the brilliantly coloured flowers are produced for weeks in early summer. But they are fussy. They hate wetness around the crown, so plant at a slight angle (to allow water to drain away) in an extra-gritty compost. And they don't like midday sun either. Having said that, they really are worth growing, and the 'Cotyledon Hybrids' (15cm/6in) are the easiest.

❋ PHLOX

The alpine varieties are delightful – low, mat-forming, long lived and

reliable. In a sunny position, and well-drained soil, they're smothered in blossom through late spring and early summer. Growing to 10cm/4in or so, they're available in a wide range of colours. Three to look out for – rosy red 'Temiskaming', clear blue 'GF Wilson' and pure white 'White Delight'.

❋ SAXIFRAGA

A remarkable family of plants, and the easiest are the mossy-leaved varieties, best in partial shade; 'Cloth of Gold' (15cm/6in) forms golden tussocks with white flowers. The cushion-forming types prefer sun but they hate getting too dry – 'Jenkinsiae' (10cm/4in) has large shell-pink flowers above tight, minute foliage. The silvery-leaved (also called 'encrusted') forms love full sun.

❋ SEDUM (Stonecrop)

Popular and easy, the rockery sedums form tight little rosettes of leaves, and most flower to no more than 10cm/4in. But avoid the common stonecrop, *Sedum acre* – it's very invasive. Grow the far better forms like

Saxifraga *'Cloth of Gold'*

'Cape Blanco' (creamy-grey rosettes and flattened heads of yellow flowers) and 'Purple Carpet' (deep red-purple leaves, bright pink flowers). Sedums do best in full sun.

❋ SEMPERVIVUM (Houseleek)

With their tiny rosettes of fat leaves and thick stalks of flower, sempervivums look more like indoor succulents, but are perfectly hardy. Traditionally grown to ward off lightning (and our pots have certainly never been struck), they need full sun. Grow the really colourful forms like red-leaved 'Commander Hay'. Most reach a flowering height of around 10cm/4in.

❋ THYMUS (Thyme)

The ground-hugging forms of thyme are a delight, producing tight 5cm/2in carpets of aromatic leaves and masses of pretty flowers. Ideal for growing over the edge of pots in full sun. Woolly thyme (*Thymus pseudolanuginosus*) has soft grey-green leaves and masses of pink flowers, while 'Bertram Anderson' forms golden mats which glow on through winter.

Sempervivums in shallow containers

ROSES

Best ROSES

❀ MINIATURES

The babies of the rose world, they are exquisite. At their tallest they're only 45cm/18in, so they're perfect for pots and will flower all summer long. Grow in sun and lightly trim over in spring to keep them neat. 'Starina' is a little star, with bright orange/red miniature hybrid tea blooms, 'Rise 'n' Shine' is a cheerful golden yellow and 'Easter Morning' a lovely ivory white double.

❀ PATIO ROSES

Some of the very best roses to grow in containers. They're compact, few growing taller than 60cm/24in, tough as old boots and flower for months on end. In fact they're as good as bedding plants for summer displays – yet unlike most bedding plants, they'll last for years. Grow in sun, in 30cm/12in pots, and clip back lightly every spring. There are some superb varieties to choose from including 'Sweet Dream' (a charmer with peachy apricot flowers), 'Gentle Touch' (dainty soft pink blooms), 'Top Marks' (bright orange/red, very free flowering), 'Little Bo-Peep' (a pretty pale pink, looking like a miniature old shrub rose) and 'Sweet Magic' (glowing orange, tinted gold, with a slight scent).

Patio rose 'Sweet Dream'

❀ GROUND-COVER ROSES

The best groundcover varieties for containers belong to the 'County' series – tough, free flowering and remarkably easy to care for. To tidy them up, simply clip them over with shears in spring. So why not take a trip to 'Avon' (double white), to 'Gwent' (double lemon yellow) and to 'Kent' (semi-double scented white). None of these will reach to more than 45cm/18in high, but they will spread well beyond the rim of the container.

❀ HYBRID TEA and FLORIBUNDA ROSES

Any of the smaller varieties will do well, ideally in 40cm/16in pots – just be sure to avoid vigorous types like 'Queen Elizabeth'. Some of the very best include 'Freedom' (the finest yellow of all), 'Sexy Rexy' (soft pink flowers, disease-resistant foliage), 'Royal William' (dark red and fragrant) and 'Rosemary Harkness' (orange/salmon, sweetly scented).

❀ SHRUB ROSES

Most of the wonderfully romantic old shrub roses aren't suitable for containers – they get too big and most have a short period of flower. But there are a few smaller varieties

Groundcover rose 'Surrey'

TIPS

✔ *All roses need deep containers in order to establish a good root system. Generally, a minimum depth of 30cm/12in is required for miniature and patio roses, and 45cm/18in for all other types.*

✔ *One of the prettiest pots we've ever planted consisted of a standard 'Nozomi' rose, with delicate pearl pink flowers on gently weeping stems, underplanted with three 'Nozomi' bush roses. It flowered for two months, looking breathtaking.*

✔ *For really low maintenance rose growing, stick to the groundcover and patio roses. They are the most trouble-free of all.*

✔ *Mail order rose nurseries, which advertise in gardening magazines, supply a much wider range of roses than the average garden centre.*

Shrub rose 'The Fairy'

that will grow happily in 40cm/16in pots: 'Little White Pet' (with masses of white pompons), 'Cécile Brunner' (thimble-sized blush pink blooms – but be sure to get the non-climbing form) and the very similar pale apricot 'Perle d'Or'. Some of the smaller English roses (see p.29) are good too.

❀ STANDARD ROSES

Lovely as the centrepiece in a half barrel, underplanted with lavenders or other roses. They should always be well staked. Patio rose standards are the most suitable, and we're rather fond of the semi-weeping groundcover standards too – 'The Fairy', with clusters of pale pink pompon flowers, is especially lovely.

❀ CLIMBERS

For a glorious display of summer-long colour, pick the repeat flowering climbers rather than the ramblers, which generally flower only once and are too vigorous for containers. Plant in 45cm/18in tubs in a sunny position. Our favourites include 'Compassion' (pale salmon-orange, wonderfully fragrant), 'Golden Showers' (bright yellow, very free-flowering) and 'Dublin Bay' (a glorious deep red) – all growing to around 3m/10ft. The new climbing miniature roses are useful too, reaching a relatively modest height of 1.8m/6ft and flowering from June through to the first frosts. The flowers are small and beautifully formed, rather like miniature

Hybrid tea rose 'Freedom'

hybrid tea roses. Especially good are 'Laura Ford' (golden yellow), 'Nice Day' (soft salmon pink, fragrant) and 'Warm Welcome' (scented orange/ vermilion blooms with coppery red foliage).

SHRUBS

Best SHRUBS

Lavandula angustifolia *'Hidcote'*

❀ CHOISYA (Mexican orange blossom)

A superb mound-forming evergreen with glossy aromatic leaves, covered in clusters of starry white flowers in June and again in autumn. Growing to 1.2m/4ft in a tub, it prefers a sunny position although it will tolerate partial shade in warmer areas, and should be sheltered from cold winds. The golden-leaved form 'Sundance' is just as lovely but slower.

❀ ELAEAGNUS

Two elaeagnus in particular are excellent evergreens for year-round colour. 'Maculata' is the sunniest, with a striking golden yellow splash in the middle of each dark green leaf. It will slowly reach 1.2m/4ft in sun or light shade. 'Limelight' is faster, slightly taller and has softer lime-green variegation which blends in well with other plants.

❀ EUONYMUS

Pretty evergreens with small, variegated leaves, thriving in sun or shade. 'Emerald 'n' Gold' is low growing, with green and gold leaves that take on a pink tinge in winter. The slightly less vigorous 'Silver Queen' is white-variegated. Both grow to 60cm/2ft. The very compact 'Microphyllus' varieties make excellent centrepieces for winter baskets and window boxes.

❀ HEBE

All hebes are evergreen and prefer full sun. Two very neat ladies, at only 30cm/12in, are 'Margret' (a profusion of sky blue flowers, fading to white, from June onwards) and 'Rosie' (bright rosy pink flowers all summer). Lightly trim in spring to keep in shape. Beware the variegated forms sold in autumn – they are tender and are usually dead by Christmas.

❀ LAVENDER

Much loved for their aromatic silver-grey foliage and beautiful midsummer flowers, lavenders grow well in containers and are a particularly good foil for roses. 'Hidcote' is one of the best – neat, compact (45cm/18in), with an abundance of dark violet-blue flowers. Grow in sun, and keep in trim by cutting back the top third of the bush each spring.

❀ MAGNOLIA

The most manageable of all magnolias for a container is *Magnolia stellata*, a compact (1.2m/4ft) rounded shrub, the bare branches covered in exquisite star-like flowers in early spring. Grow in a container on its own, in lime-free ericaceous compost, in sun or partial shade. Early morning sun can damage frosted blooms, so avoid east-facing spots if possible.

❀ MAHONIA

For real impact, grow one of the stately, tall-growing varieties of evergreen mahonia in a large container. It'll happily reach 1.8m/6ft in sun or part shade and look superb all year. 'Charity' has the characteristic spiny, holly-like leaves which are attractive in their own right, with the bonus of

Euonymus *'Emerald 'n' Gold'*

fountaining spikes of golden yellow, scented flowers in early winter.

❀ PIERIS

Wonderful evergreens, at their finest in spring when they produce brilliant red young foliage which makes a dramatic contrast with the dangling clusters of white lily of the valley-like flowers. The best variety is 'Forest Flame', growing to 1.2m/4ft. White-variegated forms are lovely, too, but produce fewer flowers. Use ericaceous compost and grow in light shade.

❀ RHODODENDRONS and AZALEAS

Tough, reliable and, for a few weeks in spring, extremely colourful. Of the dwarf varieties of rhododendron, the evergreen yakushimanum hybrids are the loveliest, growing into neat mounds

to 90cm/3ft. The Japanese azaleas are also evergreen, smaller (to 60cm/2ft) and not quite so neat, but can't be beaten for flower power. Grow in ericaceous compost and keep well watered. Best in shade.

❀ SKIMMIA

Valuable evergreens for sun or shade, with clusters of creamy white flowers in spring and, if it's a female plant, bright red berries in autumn. 'Veitchii' is the best for berries, but must be grown near a male variety like 'Rubella' which has pink-budded fragrant flowers. Both grow to 60cm/2ft. The smaller *Skimmia japonica reevesiana* is self-fertile,

Pieris *'Forest Flame'*

but lacks the impact of the other two. Grow in ericaceous compost.

Note: Other favourite shrubs for containers include camellias (see p. 29) and hydrangeas (see p. 36).

TIPS

✔ *Variegated shrubs can occasionally develop plain green shoots. This is known as 'reversion' and these shoots should be cut out as soon as they are noticed.*

✔ *For really exposed positions, in sun or shade, one of the toughest of all shrubs is* Cotoneaster horizontalis. *Ideal for growing against a wall, its fan-like branches produce a mass of scarlet berries in autumn.*

✔ *One of the most beautifully scented shrubs for a container is the miniature lilac,* Syringa *'Palibin', with masses of lilac-pink flowers in May. Grows to 90cm/3ft and is best in sun.*

Rhododendron *'Cynthia'*

TREES

Best TREES

Note: The heights given are for trees grown in containers; most would far exceed these heights in the open garden.

❀ ACER (Maple)

The Japanese maples have the lot: attractive leaves, glorious autumn colour and a neat shape which looks good even in winter. *Acer palmatum* has fresh green, palm-shaped leaves that turn deep red in autumn, and the glowing deep red form *Acer palmatum atropurpureum* is equally lovely –

both grow to 1.8m/6ft. The cut-leaved forms of *Acer palmatum dissectum* in shades of red, green and bronze, are slower growing but even prettier, to 1.2m/4ft. All Japanese maples need light shade, shelter from strong winds and must be kept well watered.

❀ BETULA (Birch)

Among the tallest of trees that will grow happily in containers, birches are especially loved for their glowing white bark. *Betula pendula* 'Tristis' has elegantly drooping

Betula jacquemontii

branches and can reach 3m/10ft or more. Dome-shaped *Betula pendula* 'Youngii' is a true weeper, to 2.5m/8ft. The upright Himalayan birch, *Betula utilis jacquemontii* has the most beautiful bark of all, but it needs space, at 4m/13ft. Birches can be grown in sun or partial shade.

❀ EUCALYPTUS

A very fast-growing evergreen for a sunny spot, with lovely blue-green foliage. We weren't sure whether to include this in trees or shrubs. It's sold as a tree but will get far too tall and ungainly in tubs – so cut it back to 23cm/9in every May and grow it as a very colourful shrub to 1.5m/5ft. The rounded juvenile foliage of *Eucalyptus gunnii* makes it an especially attractive form.

❀ MALUS (Crab apple)

Beautiful spring blossom and a colourful autumn crop of ornamental fruit. 'Red Sentinel' is tall (3.6m/12ft) but the glossy scarlet fruits last through the winter. *Malus floribunda* is an attractively domed form to 3m/10ft, with tiny yellow apples, and the smallest of the lot is bushy *Malus sargentii* (1.8m/6ft) with red-flushed fruits. Malus can be grown in sun or partial shade.

Acer palmatum dissectum

Malus *'Golden Hornet'*

✿ PRUNUS (Ornamental cherries)

Spectacular in flower but rather dull for the rest of the year, with a few exceptions: 'Kiku-shidare-zakura' (Cheal's weeping cherry) develops into an umbrella-like weeper (2m/7ft) with pink double flowers; paler pink 'Amanogawa' forms an upright column to 3m/10ft; tiny, bushy 'Kojo-no-mai', at 1.2m/4ft, has pink flowers ageing to white, and brilliant autumn colour. All ornamental cherries are best in sun.

✿ ROBINIA PSEUDOACACIA (False acacia)

Robinia pseudoacacia 'Frisia' has showy bright golden foliage, turning coppery hues in autumn. Easy to grow in a sunny position, sheltered from strong winds. It reaches 3m/10ft and can be pruned in spring to keep it more bushy. It will brighten up any patio and the acacia-like foliage won't cast too much shade.

✿ SALIX (Willow)

Tough, tolerant trees for sun or shade, but only the smaller varieties are suitable for containers. The best form is *Salix caprea* 'Kilmarnock', which makes a small (1.8m/6ft), umbrella-shaped tree with almost vertically weeping branches that are covered in pussy willow catkins in early spring. Children absolutely adore it. To thrive, it must be kept well watered.

✿ SORBUS (Mountain ash, rowan)

With clusters of white spring flower, good autumn colour and long-lasting berries, the rowans deserve to be more widely grown. And they can cope with drier conditions than most other trees. *Sorbus vilmorinii* is particularly elegant, with fern-like leaves, red autumn colour and pink berries (2.7m/9ft). Ideal for sun or shade. A slightly taller alternative is the exquisite *Sorbus cashmiriana*, bearing pale pink blossom and long-lasting white fruits.

TIPS

✔ For really tiny trees, look out for the 'patio standards' at your local garden centre, some looking like lollipops, others weeping. These are varieties grafted onto a bare stem some 1.2m/4ft high, often using shrubs like cotoneaster and euonymus. Cut off any shoots that sprout from the bare stem.

✔ If a tree outgrows its alloted space, by all means prune it. But try to retain the natural shape, rather than cutting it into a neat 'bobble'.

✔ All of the taller trees should be well staked at planting time. As a general rule, anything over 1.8m/6ft needs support in all but the most sheltered position, and smaller trees will need staking in exposed areas.

Prunus *'Amanogawa'*

Best VEGETABLES

Courgette 'Gold Rush'

❀ BEANS, FRENCH

Fresh-picked, they taste far better than anything the supermarket can offer. The dwarf varieties which reach 45cm/18in are the the easiest to grow, four plants to a 30cm/12in pot, ten in a growbag. Grow in the same way as runner beans (minus the canes) and pick regularly. 'Aramis' and 'Delinel' are excellent varieties.

❀ BEANS, RUNNER

Few vegetables are as much fun. Grow them in half barrels up a 1.8m/6ft wigwam of bamboo canes or in a growbag against a trellis or fence. They'll romp away in a sunny sheltered spot, and flower and crop prolifically. Sow seed outdoors as soon as any danger of frost has passed, keep well watered, and pick while young. 'Desirée' and 'Polestar' crop well, 'Painted Lady' has the prettiest flowers.

❀ CARROTS

Attractive ferny foliage and mouthwatering when home-grown, the early varieties are ideal for pots and even window boxes.

Sow seed in early March, and as they germinate, thin out to 2.5cm/1in apart. Start cropping in June when the roots are 13mm/½in in diameter. Round-rooted 'Early French Frame' and finger carrot 'Suko' are both good.

❀ COURGETTES

Another favourite of ours, but they do need some room to do well: one plant in a 45cm/18in half barrel or a growbag. Plant them out when there's no longer any risk of frost in a sunny sheltered spot, and don't let them dry out. Pick them young or they'll rapidly become marrows. Grow the disease-resistant 'Defender' or the decorative yellow 'Gold Rush'.

❀ LETTUCE

The pretty looseleaf (salad bowl) and cos varieties are the best, either singly in 12.5cm/5in pots, in window boxes, or twelve to a growbag. Plants are available at garden centres, but it's easy enough to sow seed in April or May. Keep well watered. The looseleaf varieties can be picked, a few

Runner beans trained to grow up canes

Potatoes

TIPS

✔ Generally, the bigger the container the better your crop will be. Avoid very shallow containers, less than 20cm/8in deep.

✔ For easy maintenance, grow several plants like peppers in one pot. One plant needs a 25cm/10in pot, whereas three would grow perfectly happily in a 45cm/18in half barrel and need less frequent watering.

✔ Try other salad crops, too. Spring onions, sown in March, can be harvested from May. Radishes mature incredibly quickly and can be ready for harvesting just four weeks after sowing. Both can be grown about 2.5cm/1in apart in 15cm/6in pots.

leaves at a time, over a long period – 'Lollo Biondi' and 'Lollo Rossa' are good. 'Little Gem' is a tasty cos.

❀ PEPPERS and AUBERGINES

Both need sunny, sheltered positions to do well and are safer grown under glass in colder areas. Grow one plant per 25cm/10in pot or three to a growbag. Pinch out the top when they reach 30cm/12in, to encourage bushiness. The best aubergines are 'Bambino' for mini fruits, 'Slice Rite' for heavy crops. The best sweet peppers are 'Redskin' and 'Early Prolific'.

❀ POTATOES

Don't expect bumper crops, but they'll taste wonderful grown in barrels about 75cm/2ft 6in deep, 60cm/2ft wide. In March, place four potatoes in a cool light spot indoors

to sprout. When sturdy shoots have developed, place them on a 10cm/4in layer of compost in the barrel and cover with a further 15cm/6in. As the shoots grow, keep covering with compost until you reach the top of the barrel. Water and feed well. Two good early varieties are 'Dunluce' and Foremost'.

❀ SWISS CHARD (Seakale beet)

Even enthusiasts like us would concede that few vegetables look totally stunning in pots, but 'Rhubarb Chard' does. It has deep green leaves with glowing red midribs. And you get two flavours – the leaves are as tasty as spinach, the midribs as delicate as asparagus. Grow one plant per 12.5cm/5in pot, from seed sown in May.

❀ TOMATOES

There's no match for the flavour (and aroma) of home-grown tomatoes and if you've got a sunny sheltered spot, they're one of the most rewarding of all container vegetables. There are two main types. Cordon varieties should be grown on 1.5m/5ft canes, all sideshoots removed and the top pinched out when the fourth truss of fruit has set. These include the delicious cherry-sized 'Gardener's Delight' and 'Sungold' and the larger 'Ailsa Craig'. Bush varieties can be allowed to sprawl, and need no tying in or sideshoot removal; two excellent varieties are 'Red Alert' and dwarf 'Pixie'. Tomatoes can be grown individually in 23cm/9in pots or three per growbag. Plant out when all danger of frost has passed. Water regularly and feed well.

Plants for special purposes

By the time you've reached this stage in the book, we hope you've been inspired to try some new ideas. This summary of our top plants might help you with your planning.

Plants for sun

BEDDING PLANTS
Alonsoa
Bacopa (Sutera)
Begonia semperflorens
Bidens
Brachycome
Busy lizzie (Impatiens)
Convolvulus sabatius
Diascia
Forget-me-not (Myosotis)
Fuchsia
Geranium (Pelargonium)
Glechoma (Nepeta)
Helichrysum
Ivy (Hedera)
Lamium
Lobelia
Lotus
Marguerite
    (Argyranthemum)
Nasturtium
Ornamental cabbages
Osteospermum
Pansy
Petunia
Plectranthus
Polyanthus
Nicotiana
Scaevola
Solenopsis
    (Laurentia/Isotoma)
Verbena

BULBS
Agapanthus
Allium
Begonia, tuberous
Crocus
Daffodil (Narcissus)
 Hyacinth
    Iris
    Lily

Snowdrop (Galanthus)
Tulip

CLIMBERS
Cobaea scandens
Clematis
Ivy (Hedera)
Jasmine
Honeysuckle (Lonicera)
Nasturtium
Parthenocissus
Passion flower
    (Passiflora)
Pyracantha
Rose
Sweet pea
Wisteria

CONIFERS
Abies
Chamaecyparis
Cryptomeria
Juniperus
Picea
Pinus
Taxus
Thuya

**FRUIT AND
VEGETABLES**
All

HARDY PERENNIALS
Ajuga
Alchemilla
Artemesia
Geranium
Grasses
Heathers
Heuchera
Houttuynia
Salvia

HERBS
All

ROCKERY PLANTS
Campanula
Cerastium
Corydalis
Dianthus
Helianthemum
Lewisia
Phlox
Saxifrage (most)
Sedum
Sempervivum
Thyme

ROSES
All

SHRUBS
Choisya
Cordyline
Elaeagnus
Euonymus
Hebe
Holly (Ilex)
Lavatera
Lavender
Magnolia
Mahonia
Phormium
Skimmia

TREES
Betula
Cotoneaster (standard)
Eucalyptus
Malus
Prunus
Robinia
Salix
Rowan (Sorbus)

Plants for light shade

BEDDING PLANTS
Begonia semperflorens
Brachycome
Busy lizzie
    (Impatiens)
Felicia
Forget-me-not
    (Myosotis)
Fuchsia
Geranium
    (Pelargonium),
    scented-leaved
Glechoma (Nepeta)
Helichrysum
Lamium
Lobelia
Mimulus
Nicotiana
Ornamental cabbages
Pansy
Polyanthus

BULBS
Begonia, tuberous
Crocus
Daffodil (Narcissus)
Hyacinth
Iris
Lilies, some
Snowdrop (Galanthus)
Tulip

CLIMBERS
Clematis, some
Ivy (Hedera)
Lonicera x americana
    (honeysuckle)
Parthenocissus
Pyracantha
    (wall shrub)
Roses, some

CONIFERS
Chamaecyparis
Juniperus
Taxus

HERBS
Chives
Mint
Parsley

HARDY PERENNIALS
Ajuga
Alchemilla
Astilbe
Bamboo
Ferns
Geranium (most)
Helleborus
Heuchera
Hosta
Houttuynia

ROCKERY PLANTS
Corydalis
Lewisia
Saxifraga
    (mossy types)

SHRUBS
Acer
Box (Buxus)
Camellia
Choisya
Elaeagnus
Euonymus
Fatsia
Hydrangea
Holly (Ilex)
Magnolia
Mahonia
Pieris
Rhododendron
    & azalea
Skimmia

TREES
Japanese maples (Acer)
Betula
Malus
Salix
Rowan (Sorbus)

Plants for heavy shade

Acer, Japanese TR
Ajuga HP
Alchemilla HP
Astilbe HP
Aucuba SH
Begonia BP & BU
Betula TR
Busy lizzy (Impatiens) BP
Box (Buxus) SH
Euonymus SH
Euphorbia robbiae
Fatsia SH
Ferns, many
Ivy (Hedera) CL
Helleborus HP
Hosta HP
Hydrangea SH
Holly (Ilex) SH/TR
Lamium HP
Mahonia SH
Pieris SH
Rhododendron & azalea
    SH
Salix TR
Skimmia SH
Rowan (Sorbus) TR

KEY:
BP = Bedding plant, BU = Bulb, CL = Climber, HE =
Herb, HP = Hardy perennial, SH = Shrub, TR = Tree

Plants for scented flowers or foliage

Bay SH/TR
Basil HE
Camomile HE
Chives HE
Choisya SH
Daffodil (Narcissus),
    some BU
Eucalyptus SH/TR
Fennel HE
Geranium (Pelargonium),
    scented-leaved BP
Hyacinth BU
Ipheion BU
Iris reticulata, some, BU
Lavender SH
Lily, many BU
Lonicera (honeysuckle)
    CL
Mahonia, some, SH
Marjoram HE
Mint HE
Nicotiana, some, BP
Oranges & lemons SH/TR
Parsley HE
Rocket HE
Rose, many SH/CL
Rosemary HE
Sage HE
Sweet cicely HE
Sweet pea CL
Lilac (Syringa) SH/TR
Tarragon HE
Thyme HE
Verbena, some, BP

Problem Solving

This sounds ominous, you're probably thinking. Just when I've summoned up some enthusiasm for the whole idea, they're going to depress me with tales of doom and gloom about all the things that can go wrong.

Don't worry, we're great believers in prevention rather than cure. If you start with healthy plants and grow them in the conditions they like, then there really shouldn't be any major disasters. Yes, occasionally things may start chomping at the foliage or a few leaves might become discoloured, but if you keep an eye on your plants and deal with any problem as soon as you notice it, there won't be any irreparable damage.

Some things are more obvious than others. Drooping leaves, for instance, are generally a sign that plants need watering. Other problems may not be quite so visible. So every time you are watering or deadheading, inspect the plants for any signs of pest or disease. Something as simple as picking off an infected leaf or shoot will eliminate a problem before it can spread any further.

THE MOST COMMON PESTS AND DISEASES
Slugs and snails
Probably the most common pest that you'll encounter. Virtually all plants are prospective snacks for them, even those in hanging baskets which you'd think would be impossible to reach. The telltale signs are nibbled, tattered or holed leaves, and in a really bad attack they can be stripped bare; often, a silvery slime trail is visible. Bulbs such as tulips may also be eaten by soil-dwelling slugs.

There are various control methods. Newly planted containers can be top-dressed with **cocoa-shell mulch** – it looks good, smells of chocolate, helps retain moisture and best of all, has a slightly rough surface that makes life uncomfortable for the marauding molluscs. **Washed gravel** can be used in the same way. But as soon as the foliage of the plants reaches the edge of the container, it acts as a footbridge for the canny creatures, so you'll have to resort to sterner measures. Slug and snail killers based on **aluminium sulphate** are effective, safe for other wildlife, but rather expensive. **Slug pellets**, though not so environmentally friendly, are cheaper. Scatter

powdery mildew

them thinly, 10-15cm/4-6in apart and replace every fortnight. Alternatively, a **biological control** using microscopic slug-killing nematodes (eelworms) is now available from garden centres. Watered in, it lasts six weeks, but isn't effective against snails.

Vine weevil
A vine weevil attack is tricky to spot at first since it's the grubs (up to 13mm/½in long, tubby, off-white with a brown head) which do all the real damage. They live in the compost, eating the roots of many plants including fuchsias and busy lizzies and often the first you know is when the plants wilt, discolour, then collapse and die. The slow-moving adult weevils are 9mm/⅜in long, grey black with a light speckling of gold, and they eat irregular shaped notches in the edges of the leaves.

To control vine weevil, look out for any grubs in the compost as you are potting up any newly purchased plants, and **squash them**. Similarly, squash any adult weevils, which tend to be more active at night. Squeamish gardeners will be relieved to know that there's also a **biological control** method – a naturally occurring nematode (eelworm) which can be watered into the compost in spring or late summer.

Greenfly and blackfly
These sap-sucking insects are much more obvious, and much more common. They attack a wide variety of plants, feeding on stems, buds and flowers which

eventually become distorted and covered in sticky 'honeydew' (a polite term for aphid droppings).

To control them, deal with any infestation as quickly as possible, to prevent a build-up. Organic gardeners use **soap-based insecticides**, or simply **squash them**. Alternatively, spray with the chemical insecticide **Miracle Garden Care Rapid** which contains pirimicarb. This is especially good because it is long lasting and doesn't harm bees and other beneficial insects.

Moulds and mildews

Grey mould can be a bit of a problem in wet seasons, producing discoloured spots or patches on leaves, stems or flowers, followed by a grey, fuzzy fungal growth and rotting. **Pick off** any affected material as soon as it is spotted, and if the condition recurs, spray with **Bordeaux mixture** or **Bio Supercarb**.

Powdery mildew is most prevalent in warm dry weather, especially if plants have been kept on the dry side. A powdery white coating appears on the upper surface of leaves and they yellow and drop. Again, **pick off** any affected leaves, spray any bad attacks with **Phostrogen Safer's Liquid Fungicide** and improve watering.

grey mould

HOLIDAY CARE

We know of someone who worried so much about how his container plants were going to cope while he was away on holiday that he actually took them with him. Whilst we admire his devotion, we think there are slightly easier ways of solving the problem.

Obviously, the simple answer is to ask a good neighbour to do the watering for you. But if this isn't possible, move the containers into the shade a few days before your departure (by doing it early, you're not alerting any would-be burglars). If you water them thoroughly on the day you set off, most plants should be able to survive for at least a week.

If you're going away for longer, then it's worth fixing up a rudimentary watering system. Place a bucket of water on blocks and cluster the plants around it. Cut some strips of capillary matting and push one end into the compost of each pot, the other end in the water. These 'wicks' will take up water and transfer it to the pots by capillary action, keeping the soil moist and the plants happy. But set the system up a few days in advance, to check that each wick is transferring sufficient water to its container. Larger pots or baskets may need two.

A more expensive solution is to invest in an automatic watering system. Garden centres sell a range of micro-drip systems for containers which can be tailored to your needs. Basically, it's a series of drip nozzles connected by tubing which gently drip water into the container. The beauty of the system is that it can be operated by mini computers that switch the water on for you at set times while you're away. Even more sophisticated are those with sensors that override the computer – if it's been raining for instance, and the compost is wet enough already. And of course, these systems can be used all summer, not just when you're away. Nice to sit back in a deckchair and watch somebody else doing the work for a change!

vine weevil

Index

GARDEN NOTES

GARDEN NOTES

GARDEN NOTES

GARDEN NOTES